Border Station Walks

*Walks from Stow, Galashiels
and Tweedbank stations*

WALK – EXPLORE – DISCOVER

Brian Gould and Forbes Shepherd

The authors have made every effort to ensure that the information provided in this publication is accurate, and accept no responsibility whatsoever for any loss, injury or inconvenience experienced by any person or persons whilst using this book.

- All maps from plotaroute.com with permission
- Quotation on page iii is from *The Life of Sir Walter Scott* by Sir John Lockhart, Scott's son-in-law and biographer (1794 – 1854)
- The following are from the works of Sir Walter Scott:
  - Excerpt on page 14 from *St Ronan's Well*, an 1823 novel
  - Excerpts on page 34 and 147 are from *Lay of the Last Minstrel*, 1805 poem.
  - Excerpt on page 88 from *St Mary's Lake*, part of the poem, *Marmion* 1808

(Images on the above pages depict various architectural elements of Abbotsford House, Sir Walter Scott's home.)

A catalogue record for this book is available from the British Library

First published in 2020
Copyright © Brian Gould and Forbes Shepherd, September 2020

ISBN 978-1-8382270-0-5

Printed by: **www.bordersprint.co.uk**

Front cover photo: Bow Castle Broch from Gala Water
Back cover photo: Chain Bridge crossing the River Tweed

In July 1832 a seriously ill Sir Walter Scott returned from a period of recuperation in Naples to Abbotsford, his estate on the banks of the River Tweed. On reaching the outskirts of Galashiels, the confused and uncertain Scott raised his head from his carriage –

'as we descended the vale of the Gala, he began to gaze about him, and by degrees it was obvious that he was recognising the features of that familiar landscape. Presently he murmured a name or two – 'Gala Water, surely – Buckholm – Torwoodlee'. As we rounded the hill at Ladhope, and the outline of the Eildons burst on him, he became greatly excited, and when turning himself on the couch his eye caught at length his own towers, at the distance of a mile, he sprang up with a cry of delight'.

John Gibson Lockhart (1794 - 1854),
biographer and son-in-law of Scott

Dedication:

To Leonard Gould (1927 - 2017)

A life well lived.

────── · ACKNOWLEDGEMENTS · ──────

As is almost always the case when creating a work of this type, the book would not have been possible without the assistance of others. Our thanks go to Archie Johnston, Andrew Gould, Jamie Livingston, Anne Claveirole, and Liz Shepherd.

CONTENTS

Introduction

The return of a section of the old Waverley rail line between Edinburgh and the Scottish Borders in September 2015 helped reconnect one of the most beautiful parts of Scotland with the rest of the UK. Long seen as a transit route to Edinburgh, Glasgow and the Highlands the line quickly helped to establish the Borders as a destination in itself. With its rolling hills, picturesque towns and ancient history, the word went out that the Scottish Borders is a 'go to' place. The Borders Railway now adds to the many opportunities available in Scotland to escape the strains of this high-tech age and find renewal and tranquillity in this unique part of Scotland.

Area covered

The geographical area covered by the 30 routes is relatively small, at just under 200 square kms. From low level station-to-station jaunts; to those that circle stretches of the local rivers; to challenging treks over high hills; to long perambulations across moorland to isolated lochs. This small area contains enough variety and challenge that you will want to return again and again to this beautiful part of the Borders.

Long distance paths

The area is covered by a number of long-distance paths including the Southern Upland Way, the Borders Abbey Way and St Cuthbert's Way (see below). Many of the routes in the book make use of these paths, particularly the Southern Upland Way. Both the Borders Abbey Way and St Cuthbert's Way are based on the religious tradition of the area and the physical legacy of their importance can still be seen in the abbeys and old monastic sites that survive across the region. Connections between these sites of course, were mostly by foot on a series of old paths and fords, a reminder when walking in the Borders that many have gone before you!

⟨⟩ The Southern Upland Way (SUW) runs from Portpatrick on the west coast to Cockburnspath on the east coast. Opened in 1984, it is 344km (214 miles) from coast to coast. There are no hill summits above 914m (3000 feet) but over 80 above 610m (2000 feet) offering some fine walking.

⚜ St Cuthbert's Way (SCW) was named after a local 7th Century saint who spent his life in the service of the church. The route runs between Melrose in the Borders to Lindisfarne off the Northumberland coast and is 100km (62 miles) long.

W Borders Abbey Way (BAW) is a circular route that includes Jedburgh, Melrose and Dryburgh Abbeys. Their heyday was between the 12th and 16th centuries before falling into decline either from the ravages of war or wider political shenanigans! The route passes through the towns of Hawick and Selkirk and is 103km (64 miles) long.

The Eildon Hills

Useful information

This book describes 30 walks from the three Borders Railway stations, Stow, Galashiels and Tweedbank. There are five walks from Stow station, eleven from Galashiels, eleven from Tweedbank and three Interstation Walks. Apart from the Interstation Walks all the routes return you to the station that you started from.

Each walk has an information box that gives its distance, approximate time to complete and total ascent in metres. There is a brief description of the terrain you will cross and a difficulty rating, based on one, two or three 'boots', with one being the easiest. The time taken to complete each walk will obviously vary according to fitness, weather conditions and a desire to linger, which we hope will be often!

Each route has a map with key points numbered to correspond with the descriptor and in some cases additional information is provided to help orientate the walker. Most walks are on clearly defined paths but not always well maintained. Where stiles are in place or some other minor obstacle that requires crossing, this is made clear in the respective introduction. Every care has been taken to ensure the descriptors and maps are as accurate as possible at the time of writing but neither the authors, publisher nor landowner can be held responsible for any injury or accident, regardless of cause.

The routes are varied, from challenging where boots and proper outdoor clothing is required to the more benign that can be walked without any specialist footwear or clothing. Please take note of the information boxes before deciding on your route.

Text boxes give information on local history, culture or folklore as it relates to the countryside you are passing through. Some walks take you past information boards where additional information can be found. Photographs taken by the authors are included and will hopefully add to the walker's enjoyment.

Abbreviations are used for the three long distance paths that pass through the area. These are the Southern Upland Way (SUW), the Borders Abbey Way (BAW) and St Cuthbert's Way (SCW). Whenever sections of these routes are accessed this is identified within the text. The waymarkers in place that indicate these walks are also identified as they add to ease of navigation.

Both OS Explorer 338 (2017) and OS Landranger 73 (2016) cover the area of the walks.

Whatever the difficulty of the route weather conditions will always need to be reckoned with and be aware that in Scotland walking conditions can change very quickly. Most of the walks take you from the three stations to high ground where temperatures can fall rapidly, and the risk of exposure increases incrementally, so please go prepared.

There is also a need to be aware of the following.

Shooting dates: Grouse – August 12th to December 10th. Pheasant – October 1st to February 1st.

Lambing: March to May.

Take extra care when a field contains cattle, particularly if calves are also present. Keep to the field side and avoid completely if accompanied by a dog.

Access rights

Within Scotland the 'right to roam' is enshrined in Law. The Land Reform (Scotland) Act 2003 established a legal right of access to most lands and waterways. A strong tradition of public access to the countryside has existed for centuries. While the law now supports this a key emphasis within the act is the onus on all involved to act responsibly. A number of walks within the book take you close to golf courses, through farms and across farmland and close to private properties. Please respect people's privacy and show consideration for the natural environment and for all those who make their living from it or make use of it for sport and recreation. The main points from the act are below and should be complied with.

Take responsibility for your own actions. Care for your own safety, keep alert for hazards and take special care with children.

Respect people's privacy and peace of mind. Do not act in ways that might annoy or alarm people, especially at night.

Help land managers and others to work safely and effectively. Keep clear of land management operations like harvesting or tree-felling, avoid damaging crops, and leave gates as you find them.

Care for your environment. Don't disturb wildlife and take your litter away with you.

Keep your dog under proper control. Dogs are popular companions but take special care if near livestock or during the bird breeding season, and always pick up after your dog.

Access rights do not usually apply to farmyards but where a right of way or core path passes through one you have a right to proceed.

Local annual events

Galashiels Braw Lads Day: Saturday nearest 30th June each year.

Melrose Festival: Third week of June.

Gala Sevens - Rugby tournament: First Saturday of April.

Melrose Sevens - Rugby tournament: Second Saturday of April.

Galashiels Walking Festival: Last weekend of April.

Stowed Out Festival: Music and arts festival held in Stow every August.

Tempest Brewery, Tweedbank. Beer festival every Spring and Autumn.

Borders Book Festival: Melrose in June.

Miscellaneous

The Transport Interchange sits opposite Galashiels station and is the main transport hub for the town. Bus services run from here and it offers train and bus information, ticket machines, showers, bike lockers and a café.

Toilet facilities can be found at the Transport Interchange in Galashiels, next to the coffee shop on Tweedbank station, and in the town centres of Stow, Galashiels and Melrose, and at Abbotsford.

History

The great Tweed valley dominates the landscape of the south east of Scotland. The River Tweed rises from wild moorland close to Moffat in Dumfries and Galloway. The valleys it flows through and the tributaries that feed it all the way to the North Sea, make up its domain. Formed by an ice – stream during the last period of glaciation the valley supports the great river as it flows south east for 156km (97 miles) to enter the sea at Berwick- upon-Tweed.

With a catchment area of over 5,000 sq kms (2,000 sq miles) the Tweed valley is a mixture of high moorland, large ancestral estates, public woodland, small distinctive towns and a sense of a 'place apart', Scotland but different, unique and characterful. It is within the valley of the River Tweed as it passes by Melrose and its tributary Gala Water, that all the walks are set.

It was up the Tweed valley in AD79 that a large Roman army advanced through the 'wildwood' before setting up camp at the foot of the Eildon hills. The impact on the local Votadini tribe can only be imagined as they gazed down on the army of Agricola from their holy redoubt on top of the North Eildon. The Romans tolerated their presence while consolidating their hold on the area and containing any threat either the Votadini or the Selgovae tribes, further west, might pose to their presence. By the early part of the 3rd century the Romans had retreated to Hadrian's Wall while negotiating peace

Monument marking the site of Trimontium

treaties with Border tribes to ensure a buffer zone existed between the new frontier and the Pictish hordes further north.

However, it was nearly 600 years later before the great monastic settlements that so changed the social and political fabric of the Borders arrived. King David 1st of Scotland was a devout Christian who brought major diocesan reorganisation to Scotland while ensuring its independence from rivals. He was instrumental in establishing the great monasteries at Melrose,

Melrose Abbey

Kelso, Jedburgh and Dryburgh. Their demise four centuries later coincided with a period of lawlessness that the Border Reivers came to represent.

This time it was not outside influence that brought change to the Tweed valley but the native inhabitants themselves. Remoteness from a weak central authority, the devastations left by war and a reduction in the influence of a well-regulated system of Wardens presaged the emergence of a lawless society. It was characterised by parties of mounted raiders who journeyed back and forth across the border to steal mainly cattle, sheep and horses. The practice persisted for three hundred years until the early part of the 17th century when the union of the Scottish and English crowns under James I saw the new king

Sir Walter Scott

take matters in hand. His appointed commission saw the Reiving society that had taken hold on both sides of the Border quickly and brutally abolished.

While great political and social forces have shaped the Borders one individual has done more in creating an image of the area than any other. Walter Scott's romantic and heroic depiction of the Borders in books such as Redgauntlet and Old Mortality, created a history that drew upon all that had gone before, including the Reivers.

By immersing himself in local folklore and Scottish history he shaped a new identity through the epic tales of derring-do that filled the pages of his books. He not only left a legacy of great literature, but he also bestowed a new romantic identity to the Borders. Less well known is the influence of Scott on the Borders economy. His wearing of a locally produced plaid, Galashiels Grey, led to a national interest in the new cloth. A small established

Galashiels Grey tartan

River Tweed
at Yair

textile industry quickly expanded to produce an array of chequered cloth that had wide appeal. By 1881 there were 20 mills operating in Galashiels alone. Clever marketing soon had the name Tweed attached to it, forever linking the area to the new cloth.

Such was Scott's fame that when the new railway line was constructed between Edinburgh and Carlisle in 1862 it was named The Waverley Line after a series of his novels. The impact on the textile industry was dramatic, allowing for rapid export of its products while allowing new material to be imported to enhance production. The line ran for 98 miles between the two cities and in its heyday, branches sprang from the main route towards Duns, Kelso and Jedburgh and to Berwick upon Tweed on the east coast. Branch lines also operated to Selkirk and Lauder, while a west bound track went to Innerleithen and Peebles.

The Tweed valley now resonated to the sound of clanging trains, while columns of emitted steam marked their passing. The well

Steam train

documented Beeching cuts in the 1960s immediately and unceremoniously removed track and trains from the whole of the Borders, making it the largest unserved area in the UK. It was a severe blow to the morale of the region, but some indomitable campaigners were determined to have a service reinstated. In September 2015 their efforts were rewarded when a new line was created, allowing services to run as far south as Tweedbank from Edinburgh. By early 2020 over two million passenger journeys per year were recorded, far exceeding early expectations of the services popularity.

This is a land that people have moved over and through; from ancient tribes to Roman legions, from galloping Reivers to hurtling trains. This is a land where workers have settled to labour and create in field and mill. The landscape lends itself to movement and exploration, its deep valleys and gentle hills challenging and enticing you in. The return of the train and the accessibility this book provides gives you an opportunity to explore this ancient landscape for yourself.

Cauldshiels Loch

"*Where the traveller is ever and anon, discovering in some intricate and unexpected recess, a simple and silvan beauty.*"

Abbotsford House

Stow

Originally known as Stow of Wedale, the village of Stow (meaning holy place) has a long association with the Christian church. In medieval times it became one of only three sanctuaries in Scotland that offered safety from prosecution. Once within the grounds of the church a fugitive could no longer be pursued and had to be dealt with by the church authorities.

According to local folklore Stow was the site of a glorious battle won by King Arthur over the Saxons. The story goes that Arthur founded the first church dedicated to the Virgin Mary with fragments of the True Cross. Our Lady's Well, sitting close to the main A7, dates back over 1000 years and the first church was constructed in the village in the 7th century. The Church of St Mary's was built in the late 15th century and can be found close to the centre of the village with the current parish church, St Mary of Wedale built in 1876, positioned on a rise south of this.

Stow was a small community until the 18th century when the industrial revolution transformed the village into a centre of industry for spinning and weaving. A rare example of a packhorse bridge sits opposite the current church and is a reminder of the village's importance in the woollen and agricultural industries in the 19th century. Today Stow is a thriving community of over 700 people, well connected by road and rail.

Stow Station Walks

Stow Station

S1: A Walk of Two Halves

Distance: 7km **Time: 2 hours**

Difficulty: 🥾🥾 **Total ascent: 196m**

Terrain: Minor roadway, farm tracks, hill paths, stile.

This walk takes you from the beautiful Lugate valley onto the broad ridge between Cribbilaw and Cottie Hill where great views of the surrounding hills and valleys open up.

1. Leave Stow station and head uphill following the single-track road as it bears left past Stagehall Farm, after 2kms you reach Lugate Bridge.

Lugate Bridge

2. Just before the bridge on your right, pass through a farm gate to join a track that runs alongside Lugate Water. As it enters a large field it loops right towards a gate on the far side, enter onto a section of track close to the river.

> Lugate Bridge is an attractive late 18th century stone structure, with a long shallow parapet, now a listed building. Sitting low in the landscape, it carried the old stage road across Lugate Water from Edinburgh to Galashiels.

3. As the path pulls away from the river look out for a large pond hidden behind the raised ground on your left, the remains of an old fish farm. Pass through a farm gate and head uphill for a few metres before joining a path that skirts the base of gorse covered high ground.

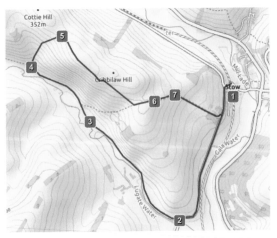

The remains of Ewes Castle are set within a square of collapsed wall at the head of the valley. Its name comes from the old name for Lugate Water, little else is known about its origins. Its position in this narrow section of the valley suggests a defensive purpose.

The collapsed remains of Ewes Castle soon appear in front of you.

4. Just before Ewes Castle head uphill on a clear track that loops the hill side. As it begins to fade, keep left and immediately join a more distinct path that goes uphill alongside a small ravine. On meeting a wire fence turn right and head up a steep section through heather. As you leave this behind follow one of the many sheep tracks towards the ridgeline on your left.

5. Quickly you encounter the wide track that runs between Cottie Hill and Cribbilaw Hill. Turn right towards Cribbilaw Hill while admiring the expansive views that open up of the rolling Border hills. When the path begins to drop you meet a walled field. Do not enter but instead keep to the clear track on your right and follow it around to your left

Lugate Valley

19

to a wooden gate. Enter and head downhill to the gate at the bottom left of the field next to a group of sheep pens.

View from side of Cribbilaw Hill

6. Head through and take an immediate left, keeping adjacent to the southern wall of the sheep pens. You quickly meet a farm track that begins the descent towards Stagehall Farm, passing close to a large communication tower.

7. Enter the next field through a small gate and head downhill on a clear farm track to arrive at a field gate that takes you into the grounds of Stagehall Farm (a working farm, so take care). Head through this to re-join the road before turning left and retracing your steps back to Stow station.

Stagehall Farm

S2: An Ancient Well

Distance: 4.5km	**Time: 1 hour**
Difficulty: 🥾	**Total ascent: 41m**
Terrain: Grass paths, stiles.	

This pleasant circular walk passes an ancient packhorse bridge and a holy well as you follow the tree-lined banks of Gala Water.

1. Leave Stow station and head downhill to the village centre. At the junction with the main road turn right until you reach a small parking area next to the packhorse bridge. Built in 1650, it was the first bridge to cross Gala Water, allowing local trade to flourish.

Packhorse Bridge and St Mary of Wedale Church

Across the road, on a rise you will see the magnificent St Mary of Wedale Church.

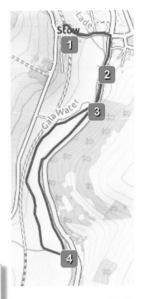

2. Beyond the bridge step over a stile and follow the path that runs between the main road and the river. After crossing duckboards, the path rises next to the river before a gate takes you into a large field. Head towards an old chimney stack that sits adjacent to a long-disused curling pond and follow the remains of an old wall away from the roadside to a wooden stile close to the river.

St Mary of Wedale Church was built in 1876 and stands above the A7 road on the southern edge of Stow. The tower is an impressive 140 feet tall and contains the church clock which had a reputation for accuracy. Train drivers on the old Waverley line set their watches by it.

3. Cross and immediately turn right towards the river and follow it downstream for about 1km on a path that runs under a long row of majestic mature beech trees. Where Gala Water meets the Lugate Water follow the bank around to a river ford that is still in use today.

4. Return by following the long water ditch that borders the field. When you reach the religious site of St Mary's Well (partly concealed by lush wildflowers in spring), a couple of steps lead down to the well. The water is only a few inches deep and crystal clear.

Cross towards the stile that you used earlier and retrace the path back to the main road and the station.

- St Mary's Well is part of Stow's religious history, dating back nearly 2000 years, one of many local religious sites.

- There was once a chapel here and a stone with an impression of the Virgin Mary's foot!

- The site was renovated in 2000 as a millennium project.

St Mary's Well

S3: A Beechwood and Straw House

Distance: 4km	**Time: 1 hour**
Difficulty: 👢	**Total ascent: 129m**
Terrain: Woodland and farm paths, minor road.	

Passing through Stow you encounter the magnificent Baronial style town hall and further on a light and airy beechwood. Muirhouse Farm is a beacon for renewable energy and has a variety of rare breeds including, Kunekune pigs.

1. From Stow station head downhill before crossing the main road with care and continue towards the impressive town hall.

2. On reaching this turn up Earlston Road taking a sharp left as the road continues to rise, passing cottages on either side.

Nuthatch

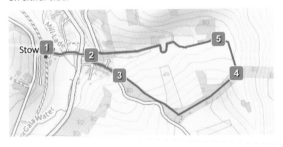

Stow Town Hall

The town hall is a sandstone Baronial style building situated at the junction of Townfoot and Earlston Road. Completed in 1885, with an entrance porch beneath a corbelled parapet. It contains a carved panel with a monogram of Captain Alexander Mitchell, a 19th century local Liberal MP.

3. As the road turns sharply right head into the woodland in front of you on a clear path. At the first fork keep left and stick to the path up this narrow corridor of conifer trees. As it flattens out you enter a large well-spaced and impressive beechwood.

Follow the path downhill keeping left until you reach a small pond and the farm track just beyond this. Listen out for buzzards calling to each other and look out for tree creepers as they scramble up and down trees.

Sell Moor Wood

Muirhouse Farm has a series of Eco Holiday homes for rent, from traditional conversions to a Straw House. The farm is organic and produces its own power from solar, wind and ground sources, helping it become independent from the national grid.

4. Turning left, you pass through a series of three farm gates before entering Muirhouse Farm. Take care between the second and third gates as cattle sometimes occupy this field.

5. Follow the track left until you reach the side of farm buildings. Do not continue up towards the main house, but take the narrow passage between the garage and barn that delivers you to the driveway below the house. Cross the small bridge, with ponds on either side and follow the track as it loops away from the farm. Pass Stow cemetery and the townhall, continue to the main road, cross with care and return to the station.

S4: High and Dry

Distance: 12.5km **Time: 3 hours**

Difficulty: 👢👢👢 **Total ascent: 326m**

Terrain: Woodland path, farm track, moorland, minor road.

The ruins of Bow Castle Broch sit on the edge of a steep drop giving stunning views of the Gala Water valley below. The cairn that adorns the site has been built from the ruins of the broch.

1. From Stow station head downhill before crossing the main road with care and head towards the impressive baronial town hall. On reaching this turn up Earlston Road until you reach a small junction and keep ahead on Hay Park Loan to where the road ends. Enter the field on your right through a farm gate onto a wide track and continue until you meet the edge of woodland.

Gala Water Valley

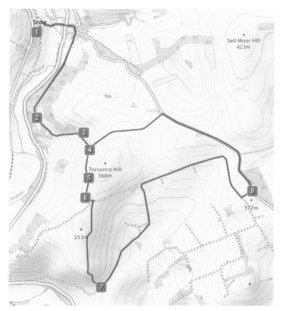

Enter through the gate and stay on the path uphill through the trees until you arrive at a farm gate. Keep ahead next to a wire fence until you reach a small exit gate.

2. This drops you onto a tarred road where you keep left past some converted farm buildings before emerging next to a cottage. Pass through a white picket gate and head uphill to a pair of field gates.

3. Take the gate on your right and follow the stone dyke up this steep section of field to the farm gate on top. On passing

through, take an immediate right and follow this well-defined farm track as it quickly gains height.

4. On reaching moorland a stone dyke with a field gate appears. Keep to the left of this and follow the wall as it drops to the corner of the field before heading to a small gate set into the dyke on your left.

5. Pass through, taking an immediate left onto a well-defined farm track. As you

Brochs are a type of drystone roundhouse mostly found in the north of Scotland. Their purpose was either defensive or an indication of a family's status. They usually occupied strategic sites and were in use for about 1,000 years from 800 BC. Bow Castle Broch is one of only three remaining in the Borders.

come to the corner of the field do not take the main track over the brow of the hill, instead pick up the less well defined but clearly visible track that lies closer to the dyke. Head past a large

Bow Castle Broch

Longpark Wind Farm

pile of stones and continue on a path that winds its away along the edge of the moorland.

6. Soon the cairn marking Bow Castle Broch will come into view. Continue alongside the wall and on reaching the field end head for the top. To return, descend the shoulder of the hilltop and on meeting a path turn right and continue down this steep descent to a roadway that services the wind farm.

7. Turn left and keep on this as it heads through the wind farm. After 3km just after a steep rise take a left turn out of the wind farm and onto the public road.

8. Turn left and continue downhill for 1.5km. When a conifer plantation appears on your left with a barn just beyond it, head through a farm gate onto a clear track. Stay on this as you cross moorland before the track begins to drop alongside a dyke and you arrive at an earlier intersection [4]. Head down the field on your right and turn left on passing through the field gate. Retrace your steps via Torsonce Woodland back to Stow station.

S5: Through the Trees

Distance: 3.5km   **Time: 1 hour**

Difficulty: 👢

Total ascent: 94m

Terrain: Farm tracks, woodland paths.

This walk takes you through the mixed woodland of Torsonce Estate and past the ruins of a Bishop's Palace next to the old kirk, built in the late 15th Century. Just beyond is St Mary's of Wedale Church, still in use today.

1. From Stow station go downhill before crossing the main road with care and heading towards the impressive town hall. On reaching this head up Earlston Road until you arrive at a small junction.

2. Keep ahead on Hay Park Loan to the road end. Enter the field on your right through a farm gate onto a wide track and continue to a field gate that takes you into Torsonce Wood. Stay on the path before passing through a stand of fir trees

Torsonce Woodland

then into an area of airy beechwood before arriving at a field gate.

3. Do not enter but instead turn left and head up a short steep path that edges the trees. At the top turn left to join a return path that leads back into the woodland. After 800m you arrive at a fork.

4. Take the left turn and head downhill quickly returning to the main path. Turn right and exit the woodland back onto a wide track. Leave the field,

■ The old kirk and burial ground has contained a church since the 7th century. The Church of St Mary replaced the original structure in 1242, with improvements in the following centuries.

■ In 1876 the congregation moved to the new church (St Mary of Wedale) on the mound just south of this site. The ruins of a Bishop's Palace can be seen over a wall to the SE of the grounds.

continue ahead and on meeting the junction with the main road turn left down Church Wynd. You pass the remains of the old Bishop's Palace before arriving at the main road used by the Bishop of St Andrews who owned considerable lands in the area during the 13th century.

Turn right and pass the ruined Old Stow Kirk and burial ground, well worth a visit. Cross the main road with care and turn left to return to the station.

Old Stow Kirk and burial ground

"Breathes there the man, with soul so dead,
Who never to himself hath said,
This is my own, my native land."

Abbotsford House

Galashiels

Galashiels originated in the middle ages as a small hamlet to accommodate pilgrims on their way to Melrose Abbey. In 1337 an English raiding party were picking wild plums locally before being set upon and slaughtered by the Scots. The town's coat of arms shows two foxes reaching up to eat the fruit from a tree, with the motto *Sour Plums*. Galashiels received its Burgh Charter in 1599, an event celebrated every summer with a local festival, the "Braw Lads Gathering", with riders on horseback parading through the town and traversing the surrounding boundaries. The town song 'Braw Lads of Gala Water' was written by Robert Burns.

The town was transformed during the Industrial Revolution using the Gala Water to power the factories and mills that established the town as a major producer of Tweed products. Visible remnants such as mill lades, a fountain and old mill buildings act as reminders of its trading past. Heriot-Watt University's School of Textiles and Design keeps that tradition alive as a world-renowned centre of learning in the luxury textile industry. This history is also responsible for the development of a permanent site for the display of the Great Tapestry of Scotland in the town from 2021.

The railway line was completed in 1849 and linked Galashiels with Edinburgh in the North and several years later with Carlisle in the South, before being closed as part of the Beeching cuts. Part of the line was reopened in 2015 and is known as the Borders Railway. It has brought significant benefits to the town and the hope is to extend the line to Carlisle, improving further the town's connectivity.

Galashiels Station Walks

Galashiels Station

G1: Bloody Deeds and Silent Pipes

> **Distance: 10km**   **Time: 2.30 hours**
>
> **Difficulty:** 🥾🥾   **Total ascent: 227m**
>
> **Terrain: Farm track, minor road, grass path, moorland, stiles.**

This walk quickly takes you to the high ground of Buckholm Hill and onto lonely Ladhope Moor. You encounter Border folklore involving bloody deeds, ghosts of the past and the strange tale of an over-ambitious piper!

1. Cross to the Transport Interchange building from Galashiels Station. Do not enter, instead follow the road right to the second of two mini roundabouts. Follow the pavement onto a bridge before immediately taking the crossing point and heading right uphill.

Buckholm Tower

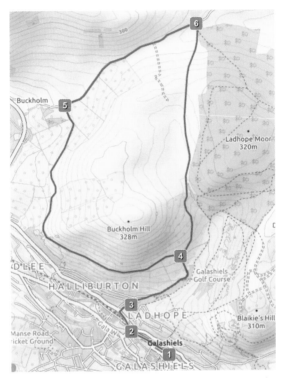

2. On reaching the Ladhope Inn, established in 1792, cross the main road and head up Ladhope Drive. After 100m cross onto a clear path next to a fingerpost that directs you towards Buckholm Circular and Ladhope Glen. Follow the path as it gradually climbs through the pretty glen then exit onto a larger path.

Track from Buckholm Tower

3. Turn left and immediately right, heading uphill through a car park next to Heatheryett Cemetery to join a rough roadway. Keep on this until joining the hill side through a swing gate next to an old transport yard and follow the track uphill.

4. Within a few metres a fingerpost directs you left to Buckholm Circular. Continue on the path as it arcs around the tower and begins to drop through fields to a minor road next to a row of cottages.

> Legend has it that the Laird of Buckholm, a cruel and vengeful man, was forever cursed by the wife of a Covenanter after he murdered her husband and son in the late 1680's. He hung their bodies from ceiling hooks, still present in the vaulted stone cellar. The ghosts of the laird and his dogs are said to appear every year on the anniversary of the killings.

5. Opposite is a fingerpost that directs you right on Buckholm Circular walk. Follow the road for 1.5 km before turning right onto a forest entrance track.

6. Take the stile into the second field on the right and head uphill to a narrow cleft in the opposite corner (path is indistinct here). Pass by a large pile

of stones (Dobie's grave) before crossing a stile onto Ladhope Moor. Keep directly ahead on the clear path that crosses this barren stretch of moorland.

You pass over a small stile and a burn before leaving the moor over another larger stile. Follow the track on the right as it winds its way around the side of the hill before returning to just below the fingerpost for Buckholm Circular you met earlier [4]. Turn left, head through the gate and retrace your steps back to the station.

Dobie's grave is marked by a pile of stones set within a narrow cleft on Ladhope Moor. He was a piper who in 1790, accepted a wager that he could play his pipes for the 10 miles that separates Lauder from Galashiels. On reaching this spot, he collapsed from the effort and died.

Cellar of Buckholm Tower - with hook!

Stile onto
Ladhope Moor

G2: A Golfing Glen

> **Distance: 5km**   **Time: 1.30 hours**
>
> **Difficulty:** 👢
>
> **Total ascent: 172m**
>
> **Terrain: Steps, woodland and grass paths, golf course, stile.**

After a steep ascent you will be surprised by the great views that open up of Galashiels as you navigate the top of the golf course. Neatly tucked into a narrow valley a course has existed here since 1884, constructed alongside the meandering Ladhope Burn.

1. As you leave Galashiels station turn left and stay on the pavement, and after passing a roundabout, head uphill.

2. At the top turn left up steps and left again. When the pavement ends cross the road and continue to where a steep roadway (Forebrae Park) joins the main road.

3. Turn right up this steep hill until the road ends next to a timber fence. Follow the path up steps and on meeting the next roadway cross and continue up more steps that run between two houses.

Roe Deer

Arriving at a small grass path turn left at the fingerpost for Ladhope Recreational Ground. This takes you to the golf club access road where you turn right uphill before passing the car park entrance to quickly reach a waymarker that directs you right across the fairway. Follow waymarkers up the middle of the course to reach a bench just above a putting green. Be considerate to golfers on this section and allow them to take their shots before moving on.

The female Roe deer gives birth to twin fawns in May or June keeping them apart for their first week and visiting each in turn to feed them. They remain with their mother throughout the winter. Young fawns stay hidden in the undergrowth, relying on their spotted camouflage to keep them safe.

4. Continue uphill, keep left and follow the path that traverses the slope. You quickly gain height before heading through a deer gate to find yourself at the top of the course where great views open up.

5. As the path flattens out and begins to drop take a left turn downhill at a waymarker, passing through a deer gate.

On reaching the bottom of the course pass through a gap in the wall before turning left onto a path that runs outside the wall boundary. Pass through a gate before continuing downhill between the golf course and Ladhope Burn, an area popular with Roe deer.

The golf course sits within Ladhope Recreation Ground, land gifted to the people of Galashiels by H. Roberts, the estate owner in 1912. Next to the club house are the remains of the 16th century Ladhope Tower. Only the basement level remains which is used as a store room for the golf club.

6. Cross over a stile onto the side of the course. Opposite is an old water well with a chain attached that once held a metal drinking cup for thirsty golfers! Follow the path (ignore the small foot bridge) to where you join the roadway from the clubhouse. Head downhill through a housing estate, turning right at the only junction and continue to the main road, retracing your steps back the station.

Ladhope Golf Course

G3: A Woodland View

Distance: 8.5km **Time: 2 hours**

Difficulty: 🥾 🥾 **Total ascent: 203m**

Terrain: Woodland and grass paths, forest track, stile.

Ladhope woodland was planted 20 years ago and sits above Ladhope Golf Course. Extensive views open up over Melrose, the Eildon Hills and south to the Cheviots as you traverse the side of the woodland.

On route to Ladhope Woodland

1. Cross to the Transport Interchange building at Galashiels station but do not enter, instead follow the road right to the second of two mini roundabouts. Stay on the pavement as it takes you onto a bridge before immediately taking the crossing point and heading right uphill.

45

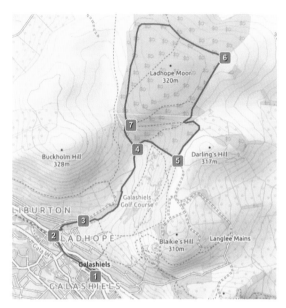

2. On reaching the Ladhope Inn cross the main road and head up Ladhope Drive. After 100m cross onto a clear path next to a fingerpost that directs you onto Buckholm Circular walk and Ladhope Glen. Follow the path as it gradually climbs through the pretty glen then exit onto a larger path.

3. Keep right, cross a small bridge on a sharp bend before taking an immediate left beside the bridge and onto a narrow path that winds its way next to a burn to the side of the golf course. Stay left and follow the side of the course to a wooden railing that guides you over a stile and into a field.

Follow the path that lies between Ladhope Burn and the stone dyke that edges the golf course.

4. After 500m pass through a gate to meet the edge of the woodland. Keep ahead, as you reach the apex of the course, cross the rough track and through a dismantled wall and head up the steep incline before you.

The dark brooding atmosphere created by the compact planting of coniferous forest prevents plants and animals from flourishing. However, fire breaks and clearings support species, such as firecrest and common crossbill. The dead wood is an excellent habitat for insects, lichens, fungi and birds that nest in openings in the decayed timber.

5. On reaching the fingerpost turn left onto Buckholm Circular path. You pass close to the tree line, with a small ravine on the other side of the adjacent wall, following the waymarkers.

Shortly a section of field protrudes into the forest. Follow the stone dyke that surrounds this. Pass through a gate before turning right and stay on the path as it curves around the woodland before meeting a forest roadway in a large turning area, adjacent to a pond.

6. Turn left and follow the roadway for nearly 2km keeping left at the one junction you meet.

7. As the track begins to drop look for a narrow path that descends right to the edge of woodland. This can be located by watching out for an old stone wall running at right angles to the roadway and an overhead power line. The path winds its way round the treeline dropping all the time until you meet the gate

you passed through earlier, next to the golf course. Turn right and head to a stile that returns you back to the side of the golf course and retrace your steps back to the station.

Ladhope Woodland

G4: Much to Observe

Distance: 5km	Time: 1.30 hours
Difficulty: 🥾	Total ascent: 200m

Terrain: Minor road, hill and woodland paths, stile.

After a steep pull up from the town you are away from the road and into beautiful countryside. The highlight of the walk is the sweeping vista of the valley occupied by Galashiels from the top of Blaikie's Hill.

1. On leaving Galashiels Station turn left past a roundabout and head uphill. At the top turn left up steps and onto Wylie's Brae. This steep ascent between large houses delivers you to Ellwyn Crescent. Head directly across to a single-track road, with a clear sign for Langlee Mains Farm (marked Private Road but open to walkers). After less than 1km you encounter a series of houses and farm buildings; continue beyond these.

Trees on Blaikie's Hill

2. Take a sharp left between two large blue farm sheds and follow the track past outbuildings until you reach a gate. On passing through immediately turn right uphill between two tree stumps. On encountering a high deer fence enter and follow the clear track. As you skirt the hilltop you start to drop to where the path meets a fenced off section of farm track.

3. Pass through the gate, turn left and enter a large field before heading to the brow of the hill where you will find the remains of an old Royal Observer Corp underground bunker. To begin your descent head towards a gate in the wall that edges a stand of conifers below this spot. Enter into a dark but short section of woodland,

Peacock butterfly

keeping ahead at a waymarked junction before exiting to an area of recently planted mixed deciduous trees.

An old Royal Observer Corp bunker sits on top of Blaikie's Hill. The Corp was disbanded in 1995 after 70 years of service. Manned by volunteers, they acted as the 'eyes and ears' of the Royal Air Force during WW2 and the Cold War.

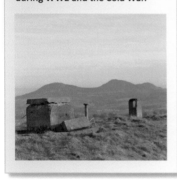

4. Keep to the grass path as it snakes its way downhill, passing a fingerpost for Gala Circuit walk. Spectacular views of Galashiels open up with Meigle and Gala Hills sitting above it and the Eildon Hills in the distance.

5. As the path swings left you meet a wooden bench. Turn right off the main path and head downhill on a grass path. As it levels out and begins to traverse the hill side, you pass through an opening in a stone dyke and within 100 metres you meet a small path intersection.

6. Turn right here and continue down this steep descent between young saplings, keeping right at any junction. As you exit these the path drops again under the low branches of an oak tree before delivering you to a wide farm track. Join the path just below this and keep right as it passes close to a row of back gardens.

Cross a small stile before meeting a fingerpost below the golf course that directs you to the High Road via Forebrae Park.

Bracket fungus

7. Head down steps between private gardens, cross the road turning area and continue down on another set of steps to the top of a steep roadway.

8. Carry on down this steep descent to the main road. Turn left and stay on the pavement for about 100m until it comes to an end. Cross to the other side and continue until you encounter the small series of steps you took at the beginning of the walk where you turn right and retrace your route back to the station.

G5: Birds and Berries

Distance: 5km	**Time: 1.30 hours**
Difficulty: 👢	**Total ascent: 200m**
Terrain: Minor road, woodland paths, tracks.	

Walk round the side of Wester Hill under a canopy of mature oak, ash and sycamore trees, keeping your eyes peeled for great spotted woodpeckers and buzzards. Under the canopy there are shrubs like holly and wild raspberry while the woodland floor is carpeted with mosses and wildflowers.

1. Leave Galashiels station and follow the pavement left until you reach a roundabout, then cross to the other side. Head uphill and continue to the Queens Leisure Centre on your right.

2. Just beyond cross the road to Ellwyn Crescent, a steep but short ascent that swings left as you reach the top. Take a right turn where a sign indicates Langlee Mains Farm (marked Private Road but open to walkers). Continue to a parking area and follow the fingerpost directing you right on the Gala Circuit/Langlee Woodland path.

3. Head through the gate and within a few metres you are directed left uphill by a waymarker. On reaching a clear path turn left and shortly right to continue uphill following more waymarkers to arrive at the top of the hill adjacent to a TV mast.

Begin your descent close to a stone wall on a path that narrows as it drops. On meeting a small path junction at a large beech tree take the less obvious left turn on a grassy section close to the wall.

Langlee Community Woodland was planted in 1997 to encourage children and families to connect with nature. It consists of a canopy of oak, ash, beech and sycamore with a shrub layer of elder, holly, wild raspberry and rhododendron. The woodland floor contains a variety of mosses, ferns and wild flowers including primroses, cow parsley, speedwell and red campion. Some of the trees are thick with lichen, a sign of good air quality.

Holly berries

When you reach an old farm gate turn right and continue to follow the waymarkers. On reaching the bottom of a steep section you temporarily leave the woodland, taking a sharp left along the side of a field and emerging next to a water facility.

Continue past on a narrow path as it loops the edge of the woodland. You encounter some unusual wooden structures including a giant xylophone and a bench made of a silver birch trunk wedged

Buzzard

between two oak trees in an area thick with holly bushes. Here you can sit and see if you can spot deer in the field beyond.

Buzzards are a common sight here where they nest on the edge of the woodland and hunt in the surrounding countryside. In the spring, to attract a mate, the male does a ritual aerial display called a 'roller coaster'. Rising high before plummeting downward in a spiral, twisting and turning before rising again to repeat the manoeuvre.

4. On arriving at a path intersection, keep right onto a wider path, ignoring a waymarker directing you left. When you return to the access roadway for the water facility, cross and continue directly ahead through the woodland.

Keep left at any junction and after 1km you arrive back at the side of the minor road. Turn left, head downhill to the main road, cross and return to Galashiels station.

G6: Redwoods and Falcons

Distance: 4.5km	**Time: 1 hour**
Difficulty: 🥾	**Total ascent: 54m**
Terrain: Woodland paths, tracks.	

The Policies are a quiet space next to the hustle and bustle of Galashiels. The woodland is home to both native and foreign tree species and was originally part of the estate of the Laird of Galashiels. Giant redwoods grace the entrance and Peregrine falcons nest in the impressive spire of the nearby Old Parish and St Paul's Church.

Entrance to Policies

1. Leave Galashiels station and head through the Transport Interchange building onto the public square opposite. Take the footbridge over Gala Water and continue to the main street.

2. Turn right and stay on the pavement until you meet a pedestrianised area. Exit left, next to the Great Tapestry of Scotland Visitor Centre (opening 2021), pass a side street before crossing the road at the next junction and heading uphill. Continue on Livingstone Place

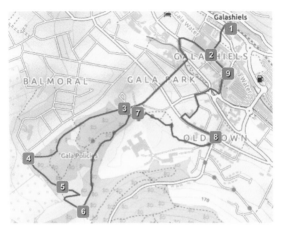

crossing a main road (Scott Street) and stay ahead until a school (St Margaret's) appears on your right.

3. Pass the giant redwoods that guard the entrance to the Policies and continue on the old estate driveway through the woodland. On meeting a fork keep right and within 50 metres turn right again onto a smaller path that delivers you to the corner of the woodland.

4. With a housing estate off to your right and a small metal bridge providing access to

> The Policies were part of the estate owned by the Laird of Galashiels and are populated by an impressive range of fine trees. The entrance is guarded by giant redwoods while the woodland contains oak trees which are more than 200 years old and were part of the ancient Ettrick forest.

Old Parish and St Paul's Church opened in 1881. Its impressive spire rises to a height of 57m (190ft) and is home to a pair of breeding Peregrine falcons who can often be seen and heard.

it, turn sharp left and join the path that runs along the top of the woodland.

5. On reaching the next corner leave the trees and follow a clearly marked path that zig-zags up a small slope. On arriving at a bench continue beyond it to wooden steps leading to the Southern Upland Way (SUW).

6. A fingerpost directs you left through the trees to a junction dominated by a large conifer. Ignore the waymarker and instead take the clearly visible path just beyond the conifer, crossing duckboards to the side of a small pond. Keep right re-joining the SUW as it runs alongside a burn before arriving at the exit point from the woodland.

7. On returning to the roadway under the large redwoods a fingerpost directs you right across a small metal bridge into the public park. Keep left and stay on the path as it winds its way across the

Old Parish and St Paul's Church

park, passing a care centre before heading out on a wide avenue to a public road where you turn left.

Old Gala House

8. Keep left at the Mercat cross and after 300m, just beyond Old Parish and St Paul's Church, whose spire is home to a pair of a Peregrine falcons, one of the worlds fastest animals reaching speeds of 386kmh (240mph) during dives. Cross and enter the grounds of Old Gala House and access the gardens through the gateway in the far corner, following the path left

Old Gala House is an impressive structure built as a tower house in 1487 by the Hopringles family. Now a museum it provides a permanent exhibition on the history of Galashiels and its people. It also contains a vibrant gallery with a painted ceiling dating from 1635.

before exiting onto the street. Keep left and quickly right past the Volunteer Hall, built in 1874 as a drill hall for the Gala Forest Rifles, a volunteer military unit established in 1859 in response to events in Europe.

A bronze bust of Sir Walter Scott occupies a prominent corner location where you cross to the public square next to a large fountain built in 1913 over the lade system that powered the local mills. A fingerpost directs you left out of the square towards the Transport Interchange.

9. On reaching Market Square you encounter a bronze statue commemorating Robert Coulter a local sweet seller who wrote the jingle 'Coulter's Candy' also known as 'Ally Bally Bee'.

Head across the square, turn left and within 200m cross, turn right, keep right towards the footbridge and return to the station.

Pond in the Policies

G7: Town and Country

Distance: 6km	**Time: 1.30 hours**
Difficulty: 🥾	**Total ascent: 153m**
Terrain: Woodland tracks, minor road.	

A pleasant easy walk through a varied woodland with stunning views of Abbotsford House and the Eildon Hills beyond. Roe deer can be spotted foraging among the trees. Gala Hill was painted by J. M. W. Turner in 1834 when visiting Sir Walter Scott.

1. From the station, cross the road and pass through the Transport Interchange building before crossing the road to the public square that leads to the footbridge over Gala Water.

As you reach the main street turn right. After passing through a small pedestrianised area turn left and follow the pavement around to the second junction.

Cross, head uphill and continue on Livingston Place until you meet Scott Street then turn left.

2. On reaching the Mercat Cross, a traditional symbol of a town's trading status and the focus of social interaction, cross over and head uphill, past the entrance to Galashiels Academy. Opposite is Tea Street which was built in the mid-17th century. Notice how the line of the roof and the eaves are constant but the ground level, door and window heads vary in height.

The Mercat Cross has occupied this site since 1599 when the town was granted Burgh of the Barony status. It originally consisted of a circular base with a flight of steps and a projecting balcony.

The road swings to the right and where a row of houses end, enter through a swing gate onto Gala Hill. Follow the path as it ascends a steep lower section of the hill before levelling out. Remain on this for 1.5km as it navigates the edge of the woodland before arriving at a fingerpost. Stop here to take in the great views towards Abbotsford House and across the valley to the Eildon Hills.

3. Take a right and return on a wider track. The woods are abundant in wild mushrooms during the autumn, while roe deer can be seen at any time. The track drops through open woodland, descending close to farmland before joining another track at the bottom of the hill.

4. Turn left here and follow the track as it loops to the rear of horse stables before emerging onto the road. Turn right and follow the road back to the Mercat Cross junction then head across to join the pavement on the left.

During autumn an abundance of mushrooms can be found on Gala Hill, easily visible from the many pathways that cross the area. Mushrooms are the fruit of an extensive network of fine threads (mycelium) that branch out underground relying on decaying matter for their sustenance.

Bust of Robbie Burns

Follow the street downhill to the front of the town library. Opened in 1873 as a free public library. Notice the carving of the words "Free Library" over the central window. Next to the steps is a bust of Robbie Burns who wrote the Galashiels town song, 'Braw Lads O Gala Water'.

"Braw, braw lads on
Yarrow braes,
They rove amang the
blooming heather
But Yarrow braes nor
Ettrick shaws
Can match the lads
o' Gala Water"

Robbie Burns

Cross the main road to the war memorial in front of the Burgh Buildings, with an impressive sculpture of a 17th century Border Reiver set before it. Behind it the names of those who died in the two world wars are engraved in bronze tablets.

Every evening at 8pm the town clock chimes out the first bar of 'Braw, Braw, Lads'.

Head over the junction towards the town centre, continue past the local cinema before crossing Gala Water.

Follow the pavement as it runs alongside the Catholic church of Our Lady and St Andrew. Within the church a side altar commemorates Polish soldiers stationed in Galashiels during WW2. Just beyond the pavement runs adjacent to the Transport Interchange and delivers you to the front of the station.

A Border Reiver

*The Eildons
from Gala Hill*

G8: Fishing Pools and Bluebells

Distance: 15.5km   **Time: 3.30 hours**

Difficulty: 🥾 🥾 🥾   **Total ascent: 279m**

Terrain: Minor road, riverside path, farm tracks, stile.

The walk takes you along the banks of Gala Water before joining the River Tweed where Sir Walter Scott's Abbotsford House, in all its grandeur, can be seen on the opposite bank. In spring the area of mainly beech woodland just beyond Fairnilee Farm is carpeted in a dazzling display of bluebells.

1. Leave Galashiels station and cross the road to the Transport Interchange building. Turn left without entering and follow the pavement past the first roundabout. Continue as the road drops to a second roundabout, off to your left is an ASDA supermarket.

Fishing hut on the River Tweed

2. Cross the road and follow the tarred path as it heads into trees with Gala Water below you on the right, a tributary of the River Tweed, that rises in the Moorfoot hills and is 34km (24 miles) long. Keep on this path as it passes beyond a car park before reaching a footbridge that takes you across the Gala Water.

3. Turn left and stay on the path as it lifts over a small rise and drops you behind a flood defence wall. Dippers are a common sight here bobbing up and down in their search for food. The elusive otter may also be spotted.

Opposite is an old mill now housing Heriot-Watt University School of Textiles and Design, an apt use considering the area's history of mills and cloth production. Gala Water accompanies you for the next km before the path ends at an old gasworks.

4. On meeting the main road turn right and follow the pavement to a small roundabout, cross directly with care, and continue under the bridge and along a tree-lined roadway. Wild garlic grows in profusion here during the early spring. Below are fine views of the River Tweed and the 18th century baroque Abbotsford House occupies a splendid position set back from the water's edge on the opposite bank.

Yair Bridge (or Fairnilee Bridge) was authorised by an Act of Parliament and erected in 1764. The single carriageway crossing the River Tweed has three arches with four semi-hexagonal pedestrian refuges to allow for a safe passage.

After 2km the minor road gives way to a path that winds its way down and up to the side of the main road to Selkirk. Keep left and the path drops again, this time passing under the main road close to the confluence of the Ettrick and Tweed Rivers before emerging at the recently renovated Old Tweed Bridge.

5. Take the wooden steps directly in front of you to the water's edge. The path now accompanies the River Tweed for 3km before re-joining the road. You pass a fisherman's hut and fishing pools with names such as Rae Weil and Arras's Putt, while

Bluebells at Fairnilee Farm

Follow the sign!

badger setts occupy sections of the riverbank. On meeting the road keep ahead to the traffic lights at Yair Bridge. Turn right and next to a cottage keep right again to follow signs for the Southern Upland Way (SUW) as it heads through Fairnilee Farm.

6. Follow the track uphill through the mainly beech woodland carpeted by bluebells in early spring. As you ascend between fields you reach a waymarker that directs you right. Keep to this track as it leaves the woodland into a field and follow the waymarkers before crossing a burn and heading uphill.

Negotiate stone steps set into the wall next to a fingerpost. Keep ahead on the SUW as it undulates across a series of fields. You pass a large cairn, created by the local rugby team during a pre-season training session! Splendid views of Galashiels sitting neatly within the valley floor appear from this point.

7. The descent takes you over a stile and into some woodland where there is evidence of the ancient Catrail earthworks. On

Cottage above the Tweed

leaving this you enter a large field and head downhill passing a spring, the source of the Moss Burn that flows towards Galashiels through woodland. In the bottom corner of the field a fingerpost for the SUW directs you over steps and onto a path that navigates the side of rough pasture to a gate in the far corner, ignoring the first waymarker directing you right.

8. You are now in an area close to Galashiels called the Policies where you follow the waymarkers for the SUW as they direct you through the trees before you exit the area next to a swimming pool. Follow the pavement right to the first junction, cross directly and keep on this street until it drops into the centre of Galashiels.

Cross the road and turn left before taking the second right into the town centre then head past the first junction and take the next left through a pedestrianised area crossing over Gala Water. Before you is the Transport Interchange building with the station just beyond.

G9: Piles of Stones

Distance: 11km	**Time: 3 hours**
Difficulty: 🥾🥾🥾	**Total ascent: 393m**
Terrain: Grass and woodland paths, moorland.	

This is a challenging walk that takes you onto high ground to the south of Galashiels, but the effort is more than rewarded with dramatic views up the Tweed Valley from the top of Neidpath Hill.

Cairn on Neidpath Hill

1. Leave Galashiels station and head through the Transport Interchange building onto the public square opposite. Take the footbridge over Gala Water and continue to the main street. Turn right towards a pedestrianised area, cross the road at the traffic lights, opposite the Great Tapestry of Scotland Visitor Centre (opening Spring 2021) bear right and continue for 300m before reaching the junction with Hall Street.

2. Head uphill and take the third turning on the right into Manse Street, passing a large public park. At the top take the single-track road ahead to a parking area beyond some utility buildings. You are now on the periphery of the town and before you lies Meigle Hill.

> Cairns have been part of the Scottish landscape for centuries. Erected to symbolise success on reaching a summit, to mark a path or to commemorate a loved one, they were once included in an ancient Scottish blessing. 'Cuiridh mi clach air do charn'. I will put a stone on your cairn.

3. A fingerpost directs you onto a grass track towards Meigle Circular. Do not go up the track that has a sign for Ben Bragge but instead enter

a field through a farm gate to begin the steep ascent to Meigle Hill. Leave this field through a small gate just below a large water tank. Take a well-earned rest here and enjoy views of Galashiels nestling in the valley with the Eildon Hills in the distance.

Wheatear

The ruin of Buckholm Tower is visible on the other side of the valley and the railway can be seen as it makes its way north towards Stow. Pick up the path beyond the water tank as it heads up hill over moorland where soon the three masts that dominate the summit of Meigle Hill appear.

Pass beyond these and descend downhill alongside the stone dyke to a gate into a large field. Very quickly you reach the end of the woodland that covers part of the hilltop. Leave the field through a small gate onto moorland and follow the indistinct path through the heather that runs next to the dyke.

Moorland route to Neidpath Hill

Neidpath Hill with the distant Eildon Hills

4. When you have reached the waymarker for Gala Paths follow one of the grass tracks to the high ground on your right. On reaching this the two tops of Neidpath Hill, adorned with cairns appear before you. Head towards them where stunning views of the Tweed valley as it winds its way towards Peebles can be had. Selkirk can be seen nestling in the valley and in the distance the Moorfoot Hills and the ever-present Eildon Hills.

There is a sheltered spot just below the first summit where you can take in the view whilst resting your weary limbs and having a spot of lunch. Keep your eyes peeled as kestrels can be seen hovering here. Retrace your steps to the field gate you passed earlier. Enter and turn right down a steep incline, on reaching the bottom keep ahead to a field gate. Pass through and follow the path beyond a pile of stones along the edge of a woodland until you meet a fingerpost.

5. You are directed left for approx 3kms following waymarkers for the SUW. As you crest the highest point, next to a large cairn, created by the local rugby team during a pre-season training

session, Galashiels can be seen below in the valley.

6. The descent takes you over a stile and into some woodland where there is evidence of the ancient Catrail earthworks. On leaving this you enter a large field and head downhill passing a spring, the source of the Moss Burn that flows towards Galashiels. In the bottom corner of the field a fingerpost for the SUW directs you oversteps and onto a path that navigates the side of rough pasture to a gate in the far corner.

'Rugby' cairn

7. You are now in an area close to Galashiels called the Policies. Follow the waymarkers for the SUW as they direct you through the trees before you exit next to a swimming pool. Follow the pavement right to the first junction. Cross and keep on this street until it drops into the centre of Galashiels.

The Catrail is an earthworks that runs all the way from Kielder Forest in Northumberland to Torwoodlee Broch near Galashiels. Its purpose is unknown but may have been a defensive structure or a boundary marker. Some believe that its existence is evidence of Pictish activity in the area.

On reaching the other side turn left, before taking the second right into the town centre. Head past the first junction and take the next left through a pedestrianised area crossing over Gala Water. Facing you is the Transport Interchange building with the station just beyond.

G10: Around the Green Road

Distance: 13km **Time: 3.30 hours**

Difficulty:  **Total ascent: 485m**

Terrain: Grass and woodland paths, tracks.

A steep ascent from Galashiels that takes you around and over Meigle Hill where there is a reminder of Scotland's turbulent religious past and an old coach road (Green Road) that once carried people deep into the Border countryside.

Access for all!

1. Leave Galashiels station and head through the Transport Interchange building onto the public square opposite. Take the footbridge over Gala Water and continue to the main street.

Turn right and keep ahead until reaching a pedestrianised area, cross the road at the traffic lights, opposite the Great Tapestry of Scotland Visitor Centre (opening Spring 2021) bear right and continue for 300m before meeting the junction with Hall Street.

2. Head uphill and take the third turning on the right into Manse Street, passing a large public park. At the top take the single-track road to a parking area beyond some utility buildings. You are now on the periphery of the town and before you lies Meigle Hill.

Looking towards Meigle Hill

The Green Road

3. Head towards the track on your right before bearing right again onto a wide flat track that continues around the side of the hill. As you approach a quarry a fingerpost directs you left onto the Meigle Circular walk. Head uphill and on entering the next field stay right and follow the fence downhill to a farm gate in the bottom right hand corner. A fence post with a directional arrow helps navigate this section. Enter the field and stay left, crossing a burn into the next field and head uphill.

On reaching the top find the gate set midway along the stone dyke in front of you. Continue on the path as it crosses the middle of this field. Exit through a farm gate onto a track that winds its way downhill, past a pet cemetery, with the site of the Meigle Pots off to your right and the village of Clovenfords in the valley below.

It was here Sir Walter Scott met William Wordsworth and his sister Dorothy in 1779 at the Clovenfords Inn when he was the Sheriff of Selkirkshire. Clovenfords housed a vineyard from 1869 which flourished for 90 years until a drastic drop in the price of grapes!

The Meigle Pots are natural land amphitheatres on the side of Meigle Hill. These were used by Covenanters, 17th century Presbyterians who refused to accept the Stuart dynasty as spiritual head of their church, leading to their persecution. The Pots acted as places of concealment where illegal religious meetings took place.

4. On reaching a junction a fingerpost directs you left, still on the Meigle Circular route. On crossing a cattle grid another fingerpost directs you right, away from the farm track and across the side of a field. Head through a farm gate next to a sheep paddock descending right on a winding path to arrive at the Green Road. This is part of a 19th century coach road that ran from Clovenfords to St Mary's Loch in the Yarrow Valley.

Garden tower

5. Keep left on this flat section before passing a small tower edging a walled garden. After you pass Caddonfoot Church follow the path as it narrows and heads left up a gorge next to Blakehope Burn, overhung by moss-laden alders. Continue uphill on a path that traverses the hill side before entering a large field, follow a sheep track up the slope to the field exit. Continue into the next field and with a stone dyke on your right begin the hard pull up to an exit gate in the top right-hand corner.

6. Beyond this gate you meet the service road for the three masts that adorn Meigle Hill. On reaching the summit a small

Caddonfoot Church

Legend has it that Wallace's Putting Stone was thrown by William Wallace against an invading English army. At nearly a metre high it is covered in moss and graffiti with the oldest dating back to 1861.

diversion can be made to Wallace's Putting Stone, an erratic boulder which sits in the adjacent woodland and can be easily accessed through the wooden gate on your right.

Otherwise, continue downhill on a rough track over moorland that eventually delivers you to the side of a large water tank, with a gate into the next field just beyond this. Head through and exit in the bottom right hand corner, but not before taking in the stunning views of Galashiels and beyond.

You quickly re-join the single-track road that earlier led you onto the side of the hill. Turn right and head downhill retracing the route back to the station.

Meigle Hill summit

View from
Meigle Hill

G11: Two Towers and A Broch

Distance: 12km   **Time: 3 hours**

Difficulty: 🥾🥾   **Total ascent: 227m**

**Terrain: Farm track, minor roads, golf course,
        footpath.**

Two ruined early 17th century tower houses with differing histories are encountered on this route and a slight detour will take you to the remains of the 2000-year-old Torwoodlee Broch, one of only three found in the Borders.

Torwoodlee Tower

1. From the station cross the road to the Transport Interchange building. Don't enter, instead turn right and continue to the second junction. Remain on the pavement as it turns left before immediately taking the crossing to the other side of the road and head right uphill.

2. Continue for a few hundred metres until you reach the Ladhope Inn. Cross the main road with care to the pavement on the left adjacent to a small car park and keep uphill.

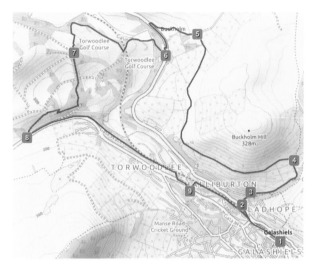

3. Within a few metres you meet a fingerpost for Ladhope Glen and Buckholm Circular, follow its direction into woodland. Keep on the path as it gradually climbs through this pretty glen to join a larger path. Turn left then right into a parking area next to Heatheryett Cemetery and exit on the rough roadway in front of you. Keep on this until you meet a swing gate next to an old builders yard that leads onto the hillside.

4. Very quickly a fingerpost directs you left to Buckholm Circular. Follow the path as it skirts the side of the hill passing through fields and after 2km or so you come to Buckholm Tower, built in 1582 by the Pringle family. Continue on the path as it arcs around the structure before running adjacent to a stone dyke that takes you on a good track to a minor road.

5. On meeting this road next to some cottages head downhill to the junction with the main road. Cross with care to the pavement and turn left until you reach the entrance to Torwoodlee Golf Course.

6. Enter and follow the road-way to the side of the golf course. On meeting the access road to the club house, take the path just behind the clear sign up an embankment to the edge of the course. You quickly re-join the roadway where you turn left to cross a rail bridge before taking an immediate right onto the course. Stay right and follow a series of waymarkers that edge the course. On reaching the far corner, next to the river, keep left and begin a steep ascent to the tee box on the highest part of the course. Just behind this you exit through a gate onto a broad farm track.

Torwoodlee Broch was built on top of an earlier hillfort in about 100 AD. Excavations in the 1950s discovered Roman glassware and pottery, possibly loot taken from the fort at Newstead. The footprint of the broch is clear and distinct.

Path to Torwoodlee Broch

7. Turn left and head downhill through trees. (Torwoodlee Broch is accessed by continuing straight ahead for 50m before turning right onto a woodland path that delivers you to the open field where the broch is located. See map insert.) At the bottom of this section head

through a gate onto a grass path, passing a small pond on your right. Exit through another gate before shortly turning right onto a broad grass track with Torwoodlee Tower before you. As the track widens take a path on your right next to an information board onto the raised ground that runs above and alongside the tower. On arriving at a small parking area turn left on a roadway out to the main road.

Torwoodlee Tower occupies a large terrace at the end of a broad avenue. The original tower fell victim to local feuding before being replaced by a new edifice in 1601. Abandoned by the Pringle family in 1783 recent restoration has helped preserve the structure.

8. Turn left and continue until the pavement pulls away from the roadside. Within a few metres Gala Water appears below you on the left and the path joins the side of the railway line. Continue to where it drops to the side of the road next to a rail bridge. Turn right and head towards the main road, on meeting it turn left.

9. Within a hundred metres cross back over the river on a white metal bridge. Just beyond take a path that runs between gardens to re-join the side of the railway track. Keep to this as it passes some large stores, eventually arriving in a parking area next to a distinctive apartment block. Head through the gap in the wall and stay right before crossing the main road and returning to the station.

Torwoodlee Estate

"And silence aids, though the steep hills,
Send to the lake a thousand rills;
In summer tide, so soft they weep,
The sounds but lulls the ear asleep."

Abbotsford House

Tweedbank

Tweedbank, as the name suggests, sits adjacent to the River Tweed and is about 500m downriver from Abbotsford House. A medieval bridge once crossed the river close to here, carrying pilgrims on the 'Sanctuary Road' to Soutra Hospital high in the Lammermuir Hills.

The village of Tweedbank began in the early 1970s as a satellite development for Galashiels on the land of a farm whose original house still stands. It has a population of over 2000, with its own school, shop and restaurant.

The area also boasts an all-weather sports complex, football and hockey pitches, and the Tempest Craft Brewery. From its humble beginnings in a garage in Christchurch, New Zealand, the brewery produces a wide range of excellent craft beers and each year hosts a Springfest and Oktoberfest beer festival.

Gun Knowe Loch is a shallow artificial body of water, providing a picturesque focus for the village. There is a small wooded island in the loch which is a haven for wildfowl including ducks and swans. The pupils of Tweedbank Primary School have created a nature trail around the loch.

The Borders Railway terminates here and its arrival has seen increased development plans for the area with a new hotel and retail outlets planned.

Tweedbank Station Walks

Tweedbank Station

T1: An Ancient Crossing

Distance: 3km   **Time: 45 minutes**

Difficulty: 🥾   **Total ascent: 29m**

**Terrain: Minor road, riverside path, steps,
        footpath.**

A short pleasant walk through the Lowood Estate following part
of the Borders Abbey Way along the banks of the River Tweed.
Look out for herons and otters and signs of an ancient river
crossing that carried the Sanctuary Road north to Soutra Hospital.

1. On leaving the platform at Tweedbank station turn left and
follow a path that runs between the car park and its entrance
road towards a line of trees. Cross and descend to a roadway that
runs alongside the wall of the Lowood Estate. Turn right and after
400m you encounter a narrow opening in the wall on your left.

River Tweed at Lowood

The medieval bridge, constructed by monks from Melrose Abbey, carried the Sanctuary Road between Soutra Aisle Hospital, founded in 1164 in the Lammermuir Hills, over the moor to the Abbey at Melrose. A wooden drawbridge would be lowered from the central tower, where the bridge keeper stayed, to allow people and goods to cross the river.

2. Head down the steps and follow the fingerpost for the Borders Abbey Way into Lowood Estate. As the small white railings end, turn right and take a winding path through trees to the riverside.

As you head upstream, Jacob sheep occupy the field on your left, further on a stone bluff can be seen on the opposite bank that once supported a medieval bridge, used by monks from nearby Melrose Abbey. There are plenty of herons to see on this stretch of the river and you may see the shy and elusive otter. Look out also for the unmistakable azure blue and metallic copper of the kingfisher as it darts along the riverbank. After 1km the Redbridge Viaduct appears (built in the late 1840s to carry the Waverley line), follow the path under the archway.

3. Just beyond, a fingerpost for the Southern Upland Way directs you up wooden steps to join a path that runs next to the railway line, stay right and follow the signs back to the station.

Stone bluff

Jacob sheep

Grey Heron

T2: A Birds' Paradise

Distance: 3km   **Time: 45 minutes**

Difficulty: 🥾   **Total ascent: 18m**

Terrain: Paths, roadway, lochside footpath.

Gun Knowe Loch is a shallow artificial body of water forming a picturesque focus for Tweedbank. The small wooded island in the loch provides a haven for breeding ducks and swans.

1. From the platform at Tweedbank station turn right to the entrance roundabout and follow the pavement to the pedestrian crossing. Cross, turn left and within 10 metres join a path that heads right into trees. Keep on this until you exit

Gun Knowe Loch

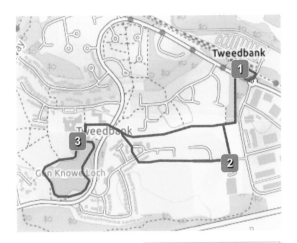

the trees and drop right to a small path intersection. Turn left to shortly arrive at a roadway adjacent to the entrance for Tweedbank Sports Complex.

2. Turn right and head past some houses. The roadway narrows to a broad path that quickly drops right before crossing a road, with metal safety barriers on either side. Continue ahead to a pedestrian underpass, head through

The loch contains an abundance of bird life, including mallard, tufted duck, mute swans, coots and moorhens. Their presence is assured by the steady supply of food provided by visitors.

Tufted Duck

and just beyond the local shop turn left out to the side of the loch. It is worth lingering on one of the many seats to observe the varied bird life.

Mute Swan

Follow the side of the loch to arrive at the front of 'Herges on the Loch', an excellent refreshment stop. Head past the main entrance and re-join the path you took earlier.

3. Turn right and head back through the underpass. Do not follow the sign that directs you towards the station, instead keep ahead, staying left at a path intersection before dropping onto a timber-edged path into scrubland at the rear of the estate.

Just beyond the next path intersection, head up a slope before turning left onto the tree-lined path you took earlier and return to the station.

Moorhen

T3: In the Footsteps of Scott

> **Distance: 7km**   **Time: 1.30 hours**
>
> **Difficulty:** 👢   **Total ascent: 103m**
>
> **Terrain: Woodland and riverside paths,
>   footpaths.**

**The Abbotsford Estate was purchased by Sir Walter Scott in 1811
and the house completed in 1824. Scott was a great collector of
artefacts and many curiosities can be viewed in the house and
gardens. Abbotsford was named after a nearby crossing of the
River Tweed used by monks from Melrose Abbey.**

1. To begin, leave the platform at Tweedbank Station, turn right
past the bicycle shed and immediately join the path that runs
alongside the railway.

Abbotsford House

2. After 1km, before the bridge turn left down steps to join the Borders Abbey Way. Keep ahead and within a few metres a path drops right to the side of the River Tweed.

Passing close to the water you traverse duckboards before pulling away from the river over a small footbridge.

Scott immersed himself in the designing and decoration of Abbotsford House. While an antiquarian he appreciated modern comforts and had a water closet installed, bells worked by air pressure and even a private gasworks to provide lighting.

On meeting a fork in the path stay left and continue away from the river to join a tarred path. Keep ahead and with the main road in sight, stay on the path as it drops under the road bridge.

An estate visitor

On the other side, head downhill into the grounds of Abbotsford House.

3. At the bottom turn right and almost immediately left onto a field track that takes you towards the river. On meeting a well-constructed path, keep right and follow the arc of the river until it leaves the riverside and enters woodland. There is an abundance of orchids and butterflies in this area during the summer. Head up the slope through the trees with views of the River Tweed opening below you.

4. As the path meets the end of the estate it turns back on itself but at a higher elevation. Follow this through mature mixed woodland and look out for nuthatches and treecreepers.

Path intersection

During the spring and summer the whole estate is full of birdsong.

On arriving at Abbotsford House continue alongside the walled garden, emerging close to the Visitor Centre and Ochiltrees Cafe.

The house contains an impressive collection of historic relics and a library with a large number of rare volumes. The walled gardens are much as Scott designed them. The Visitor Centre provides a permanent exhibition on the life of Sir Walter Scott.

Scott's literary output often obscures how physically robust and active he was, particularly in his early years. Lameness restricted him but he achieved his equality with others on horseback. From his unbounded enthusiasm for the Edinburgh Light Dragoons as a young man to riding the Border hills on his mare Sybil Grey. In his later years his health and vigour was sustained by hours of riding.

Head towards the car park beyond the centre and follow the path as it drops to a roundabout. Cross the main road with care before turning right.

5. After a couple of hundred metres, just before a large 'Welcome to Tweedbank' sign, cross the road to a small gate with a fingerpost that directs you onto the Solway Woodland Trail. Stay on this path as it winds its way through the trees close to housing and playing fields. Avoid any diversions, instead continue on the main path for 1km to a grassy area next to an industrial estate.

6. Pass the large rocks that edge the road and turn left. There is no pavement here so stay on the grass verge until you reach the main road with the station directly ahead.

Abbotsford Estate

T4: Get in the Swing

Distance: 5.5km **Time: 1.15 hours**

Difficulty: 🥾 **Total ascent: 55m**

Terrain: Riverside and tarred paths, footbridge.

Spectacular views of the River Tweed and the Eildon Hills are to be had as you explore both banks of this mighty river before crossing it over a chain bridge, its notorious 'swing' long gone!

1. Starting from the platform at Tweedbank station cross the road and follow the sign for Melrose Link path. On reaching a metal barrier, keep ahead and pick up signs for the Southern Upland Way (SUW) on your left. Pass through a small parking area, cross the road and take the path downhill as indicated by a fingerpost for the SUW and Borders Abbey Way (BAW).

Fishing on the River Tweed

2. On meeting the river head downstream for over 1km on a lovely grass path before exiting the field on your right through a kissing gate. Turn left and within a few metres follow the fingerpost for the SUW on a path that climbs uphill, taking you high above the river with great views of the River Tweed as it loops past Melrose. You pass the rear of some large houses before arriving in the grounds of the local Parish Church. Built in 1810 and dedicated to St Cuthbert, it replaced the Melrose Abbey as a place of worship.

Drop back to the riverside next to a large cauld that once diverted water to the nearby Abbey Mill, which provided the abbey bakehouse with flour. Take the path on your right as it crosses a field towards the chain bridge. The house next to the bridge is the original toll house. The door faced the bridge to allow the toll keeper to see those crossing.

> The River Tweed is one of the world's great salmon fisheries and the fourth longest river in Scotland, with more fish caught through fly fishing than any other in Britain. Such was the abundance of salmon during Victorian times that much of today's fishing tackle was first developed here.

Be thankful you are not required to use stilts to cross the river! The payment demanded to use the chain bridge when first erected in 1826 prevented many from doing so. Instead they crossed on stilts – without charge!

3. Cross the chain bridge, take an immediate left and follow the path that runs close to the water's edge where the bank is fringed with alder, aspen and willow.

After 1.5km the path widens as it heads up a slope next to a small retaining wall. On reaching the road, turn left and stay on the pavement until you meet Lowood Bridge just beyond the first junction.

4. Keep to the right-hand side as you cross the bridge with care and take the wooden steps just beyond the entrance to Lowood Estate. Lowood Bridge is known locally as the Bottle Bridge as it is said that a bottle containing newspapers and coins was inserted into the structure when built in 1826.

On reaching the top of the steps turn right and within 400m take a path left back into Tweedbank station.

River Tweed near Melrose

T5: Monks and a Kingly Kidnap

Distance: 7km	**Time: 1.30 hours**
Difficulty: 🥾	**Total ascent: 56m**
Terrain: Minor road, riverside path, footpath.	

Melrose Abbey is a magnificent ruin on a grand scale and it is believed that the heart of Robert the Bruce is buried in the grounds. The walk passes through the now redundant Melrose Station and continues along a section of the old Waverly line to the picturesque Darnick village with memories of a famous local battle.

1. On leaving the platform at Tweedbank station cross the road and follow the sign for Melrose Link path. On reaching a metal barrier keep ahead and follow a sign for the Southern Upland Way (SUW) on your left. On reaching a small parking area, cross the road and take the path downhill as indicated by a fingerpost

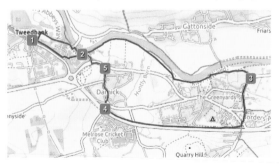

Skirmish Hill gained its title following a fracas in 1526. A local lord with some 600 mounted followers made an unsuccessful attempt to kidnap the 14-year-old King James V as he made his way north to Edinburgh. Escaping capture, the young king watched the ensuing battle from the ramparts of nearby Darnick Tower.

for the SUW and Borders Abbey Way (BAW). You pass Skirmish Hill, the site of a historic battle, where an information board provides detail on where the two forces first locked swords.

2. On meeting the river head downstream for over 1km along a lovely grassy section before exiting the field on your right through a kissing gate. Turn left and within a few metres follow the fingerpost for the SUW on a path that climbs uphill, providing great views of the River Tweed as it loops past Melrose.

You pass the rear of some large houses before arriving in the grounds of the local Parish Church, built in 1810 it is dedicated

Melrose Abbey

Melrose Abbey was established in 1136 by David I, the first Cistercian Abbey to be built in Scotland and dedicated to the Virgin Mary. It was largely destroyed by Richard II's English army in 1385. Robert the Bruce's heart is believed to be buried in the chapter house. The exterior of the abbey is decorated in unusual gargoyles including hobgoblins, cooks with ladles and bagpipe-playing pigs!

to St Cuthbert and replaced Melrose Abbey as a place of worship. You drop back to the riverside next to a large cauld that once diverted water to the nearby Abbey corn mill. Take the path on your right as it crosses a field towards a chain bridge. Head past the cottage adjacent to this and follow the single-track road. The cottage is the original toll house: it faced the bridge so the toll keeper could see people crossing.

3. When you arrive at the main road cross to the pavement, turn right and head into the centre of Melrose passing the ruins of the impressive Melrose Abbey. The Border Abbeys were centres of learning for the area's political, economic and cultural life.

Throughout its working life Melrose Abbey was much favoured by royalty. Melrose has been inhabited for thousands of years and has a wide mix of buildings. Keep left along Abbey Street into the town square, and cross to the far side.

Abbey gargoyle

Melrose Station

Take the road uphill, turn right into Palma Place and head towards the old Melrose railway station, now an Italian restaurant, built in the style of a Jacobean house with a shapely gable and tall octagonal chimneys.

Continue up through the archway to the old platform which still retains its awning, cast iron columns and detailed woodwork, before joining the tarred path that runs adjacent to the main road, following the route of the former Waverley line. The path

Facts about Melrose

■ Rugby sevens were founded by Melrose Rugby club in 1883.

■ JMW Turner painted scenes of the town and its surroundings during a visit in 1831.

■ The Mercat Cross was a symbol of the town's trading status but also used as a site for proclamations and the punishment of criminals.

■ The clock above the Ormiston Institute in the town square dates from 1892 and is dedicated to the physician and surgeon John Meikle. The building contains a permanent exhibition on the Roman fort at Trimontium.

■ Darnick Tower was built in 1425 and from the safety of its battlements the teenage King James V watched while the Scott and Douglas clans fought over his custody at Skirmish Hill in 1526.

■ The tower was destroyed in 1545 and rebuilt in 1569. Until recently it had been in the same family for nearly 600 years. Sir Walter Scott was a frequent visitor and greatly admired the tower, wanting to purchase it but the owner John Heiton refused.

drops away from the roadside before crossing a minor road and ending close to an underpass.

4. Turn right into Darnick village and continue to the main road. Cross and take the pavement left through the village. You pass the village hall and Darnick Tower, considered to be the finest remaining example of a Borders Peel tower. On meeting the next junction re-cross the main road and follow the pavement past

the junction to the crossing point then head over both carriageways with care.

5. Turn left and at the next junction cross and keep right to the small parking area you passed through earlier, retracing your steps back to the station. Darnick Tower

Old Melrose Station

T6: Damsels and Butterflies

Distance: 11km	**Time: 2.30 hours**
Difficulty: 👢 👢	**Total ascent: 223m**
Terrain: Farm tracks, minor road, stiles.	

This walk takes you onto high ground above Gattonside and past a series of pretty lochs which attract a variety of bird life throughout the year.

1. On leaving the platform at Tweedbank station turn left and continue ahead on the path that runs between the car park and its entrance road towards a line of trees. Cross and descend to a roadway that runs alongside Lowood Estate. Turn right and continue ahead for 400m keeping your eyes peeled for a narrow opening in the wall on your left.

Head down the steps and cross the bridge with care. Turn right at the cottage adjacent to the bridge and follow the pavement towards Gattonside.

2. After passing several houses on your left, follow the fingerpost for the Southern Upland Way (SUW) as it directs you left uphill on a rough track between fields.

On reaching the road stay ahead and continue on this

Red Campion

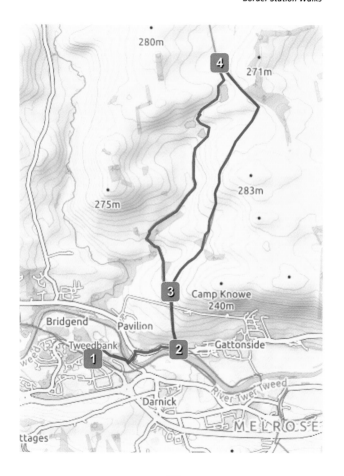

winding road ignoring signs for the SUW before arriving at a metal gate just beyond some houses.

3. Head through this and keep on the track as it heads uphill around two small private man-made fishing lochs (Byre Lochs).

Look out for a variety of bird life on both lochs. Mallard and heron are common and during the spring and autumn, greylag geese rest here during their migratory cycle.

Both lochs are well stocked with carp, bream and roach, while brightly-coloured damselflies and dragonflies are abundant at the water's edge during the summer months.

Common Blue Damselfly

Byres Loch

Return path on Southern Upland Way.

The Southern Upland Way occupies a long section of this route. These uplands were formed 400 million years ago by rocks pushed up from the seabed by the collision of tectonic plates. You have been walking on an ancient ocean floor!

The path levels out and soon another expanse of water, Stoney Knowe Moss, appears below you on the right. It is a perfect environment for a variety of plants and insects. Lapwings are a common sight here, also known as peewit in imitation of its display call. This familiar bird has suffered significant decline recently and is now a Red List species.

4. Join the SUW at a fingerpost as the long-distance path arrives across farmland from Lauder heading towards Melrose.

Take a sharp right and follow the track across moorland next to a wall. A concrete stile takes you into a large field. Keep right and follow the path next to the fence line as it drops downhill.

Painted Lady butterfly

A variety of butterflies, including the Painted Lady, can be seen flitting between the thistle flowers, a favourite nectar source for them.

Waymarkers for the SUW guide you on this section before you leave a field onto an old roadway that decends between fields edged by beech hedges and hawthorn bushes. Keep right at a fingerpost, staying on the SUW.

Re-join the road and at the first junction continue directly downhill on the same track you used earlier. On meeting the main road turn right and retrace your route back to Tweedbank station, taking care when crossing Lowood bridge.

T7: Where Legions Dare to Tread

Distance: 14km **Time: 3 hours**

Difficulty: 🥾🥾 **Total ascent: 178m**

Terrain: Riverside path, minor road, farm track, stile.

Trimontium means three hills and is named after the nearby Eildons. It was an advance Roman post and at the height of its occupation 1500 legionnaires were stationed here. No visible signs remain but numerous information boards provide details and artists impressions of this once massive camp sitting above the River Tweed.

1. On leaving the platform at Tweedbank station cross the road and follow the sign for Melrose Link path. On reaching a metal barrier, keep ahead and pick up signs for the Southern Upland Way (SUW) on your left. You pass the Scottish Public Pensions Agency, an environmentally-friendly building with a sedum roof.

Cauld near Melrose

At a small parking area, cross the road and take the path downhill as indicated by a fingerpost. Stay on both the SUW and Borders Abbey Way (BAW) as you pass Skirmish Hill, the site of a Royal kidnap attempt in 1562.

2. On meeting the river head downstream for over 1km before exiting the field on your right through a kissing gate. Turn left and within a few metres follow the fingerpost for the SUW on a path that climbs uphill, taking you high above the river with great views of the Tweed as it loops past Melrose. You pass the rear of some large houses before arriving in the grounds of the local Parish Church.

Battery Dyke

Built in 1810 and dedicated to St Cuthbert it replaced Melrose Abbey as a place of worship. Continue down steps to a large impressive cauld that once diverted water from the river to power the mill wheel at nearby Abbey cornmill providing the Abbeys bakehouse with flour. Take the path on your right as it crosses a field towards a chain bridge. Head past the old toll cottage adjacent to this and follow the single-track road.

3. Just beyond the first rise access the field on your left through a wooden gate. Cross this field and join a path that runs alongside the river where you encounter the Battery Dyke, a wall built by monks to keep the flood waters away from the fields between the Abbey and the Tweed where they grew their food. The dyke can be walked on but is narrow and slippery when wet. On reaching a series of steps head into a field and follow the loop of the river for about 1km.

Rhymer's Stone

Cross a set of duckboards after which the path begins to pull away from the riverside towards the village of Newstead. This area, known as the Eddy which is now a meadow, was once a deep pool on the Tweed. A roadway takes you through some buildings before meeting the main road.

4. Opposite on the right is Claymires Lane. Head up this past some pretty cottages and on reaching the top turn right. Within a few metres bear left and pass under an old rail bridge (once part of the Waverley line) and the road, keeping to the right of the metal barrier. At the top of the slope stay left and left again as you pass through a large farm gate onto a track that runs uphill between horse paddocks. Signs tell you not to feed the horses as they have delicate tummies!

On reaching the road turn left, where you shortly encounter a stone dedicated to Thomas the Rhymer, a local 13th century

Where the stone to Thomas the Rhymer sits a tree once stood. Under this Thomas sat to admire the view until led away to Fairyland by the Queen of the Fairies after she dared him to kiss her! Which he must have done!

laird. He had a reputation for prophecy and supernatural powers said to rival those of Merlin the Welsh Wizard. Sir Walter Scott was an enthusiast for the work of Thomas the Rhymer and published several of his works.

5. Next to the stone is a narrow gravel path with a fingerpost directing you to Newstead. Follow this until you meet a wooden bench, ideal for a short break and spot of lunch, it provides excellent views towards Earlston and the Black Hill above it.

Continue downhill and with care cross the Melrose by-pass and into Broomhill Farm. Within a few hundred metres as the ground rises you pick up the route of the old Waverly line, indicated by a Melrose Paths waymarker, as it heads into an avenue of trees.

Pass under a stone bridge, part of the old Waverley line, before arriving at a viewing platform overlooking the Trimontium site.

Access the field to the left over a stile and head right downhill to meet the road.

6. To your right is the impressive Leaderfoot Viaduct. Turn left uphill on a stretch of unused road that passes through the old Roman

Waverley Line Bridge

camp. A large plinth, the Trimontium stone, commemorates the camp and information boards can be found along the route.

7. On meeting the main road turn right into Newstead, limited pavements here so take care. As the road forks at the end of the village take the left turn uphill onto Dean Road. Within a few metres a waymarker directs you right past some stables and onto the BAW.

Trimontium is the name of the Roman fort at the bottom of the Eildons, meaning three hills. It was an advanced post of the Roman Empire and located a long way north of Hadrian's Wall. It guarded the crossing of the River Tweed and was the capital of Southern Scotland. It was occupied intermittently from 80 – 211 AD and at its height contained more than 1500 soldiers and a smaller civilian population lived in the settlement. The fort contained annexes, a bath house and an amphitheatre that could hold between 1,000 – 2,000 people.

Trimontium viewing platform

This takes you alongside fields into Priorswalk, a housing estate to the east of Melrose. Keep right and after a few hundred metres a sign directs you onto a path that passes through a park that borders Melrose Abbey.

8. On meeting the main road turn right immediately and head out of the town. As the road swings sharply right, cross and head down Chain Bridge Road.

> The Leaderfoot Bridge was built in 1863 and carried the Berwickshire railway all the way to the coast. With 19 spans, it sits 38m above the River Tweed. It closed to passenger traffic in 1948 after severe flooding damaged the line.

Cross the chain bridge then take an immediate left and follow the path that runs close to the water's edge. Head upstream along the bank which is fringed with alder, aspen and willow.

Leaderfoot Viaduct

The path widens as it heads up a slope next to a small retaining wall. Turn left and continue until you meet Lowood Bridge. Built in 1826, it is said that a bottle containing newspapers and coins was inserted into the stonework. It is known locally as the Bottle Bridge.

9. Keep to the right-hand side as you cross the bridge with care and head up the wooden steps just beyond the entrance to Lowood Estate. On reaching the top turn right and within 400m take a sharp left onto the narrow path back into Tweedbank station.

T8: An Eildon Crossing

Distance: 14km	**Time: 3.30 hours**
Difficulty: 👢👢👢	**Total ascent: 320m**

Terrain: Tarred path, minor road, woodland track, hill paths, wooden steps.

This walk has lots to retain your interest whilst providing a serious physical challenge as you loop between the Eildon Hills. You are reminded of the old Waverley line as you pass through Melrose, before visiting Newstead, the oldest inhabited village in Scotland.

1. On leaving the platform at Tweedbank station cross the road and follow the sign for Melrose Link path. On reaching a metal barrier, turn right and cross the road that passes through Tweedbank before turning left to the second crossing point at

> Newstead lays claim to be the oldest inhabited village in Scotland. It was also known as a village of stonemasons in the middle ages, likely deriving its raw material from the abandoned Roman fort at Trimontium, which helped build Melrose Abbey.

the roundabout that takes you over both carriageways. Stay on the pavement as it heads under a bridge to the underpass outside the local hospital

2. Head through taking an immediate right turn onto a path signposted for Melrose. Cross a minor road with care and follow the path on the line of the old Waverley route to the well-preserved but no longer used Melrose station. Despite its age it retains its awnings, cast iron columns and detailed woodwork.

On reaching the middle of the platform follow the steps down through an archway to a small car park. Turn right then left into Melrose town square before leaving on the narrow road on the far right that leads to Melrose Abbey.

3. On reaching the Abbey take the path signposted for Priorswalk as it runs alongside the impressive ruins. On leaving a public park, keep left into a housing estate, and pick up signs for the Borders Abbey Way (BAW). Just beyond a row of garages, follow the waymarkers for the BAW onto a narrow path and continue until you meet a stable block. You join the public road in Newstead, the oldest inhabited village in Scotland, before turning left downhill.

Don't feed the horses!

4. After a few metres head uphill still on the BAW. Keep right at the top and pass under both an old rail bridge for the Waverely line and an underpass, keeping to the right of the metal barrier.

Old water pump

At the top of the slope stay left and left again as you pass through a large farm gate onto a track that runs uphill between horse paddocks. Race horses are cared for in the adjoining paddocks with signs telling you not to feed them as they have 'delicate tummies'. On reaching this closed section of road turn left and head uphill where the road drops and rises again past farm buildings.

Looking towards Eildon North Hill

Black Hill above Earlston

5. Just beyond, a fingerpost directs you right towards the Eildons. At the first junction turn right again and continue following waymarkers for the Eildon Hills, uphill through a mixed woodland with an abundance of summer wild flowers, including orchids. On reaching the first crest you pass a wooden seat that provides great views across the valley to the Black Hill above the village of Earlston. Don't enter through the gate but remain on the track as it continues through the trees.

6. After 1km the path drops left to a small junction. Turn right and within 100m you join St Cuthbert's Way (SCW). Stay right again and leave the woodland through a gate and head in the direction of the saddle between the main Eildon Hills.

Before you arrive at the saddle waymarkers for the BAW direct you right then quickly left onto a path that runs next to a small quarry before cresting the rise and beginning its descent. On the hillside to your right earthworks can be seen that remind you of the ancient occupants of the Eildons.

Eildon North Hill

Follow this well constructed path as it winds its way downhill and keep right when the path divides before reaching an exit gate next to a fingerpost.

Head left through a gate and stay on this path as it passes between large fields arriving at wooden steps that deliver you to the side of the road, turn right downhill into Melrose. On reaching Melrose square head to the Abbey Road exit on the far side and continue past the Abbey where you re-join the BAW.

■ The remains of the largest hill fort in Scotland are still visible on Eildon Hill North. The fort was occupied from the Bronze Age by the Selgovae tribe and contained about 300 huts with up to 2000 people living there at times.

■ The Romans arrived in 79AD and established a two-storey signal tower on the hilltop. It could be seen for miles and was used for sending long range messages.

7. At the first bend turn left down Chain Bridge Road to the bridge. Do not cross but instead take the path across the field on your left, leave through a gate and head up the embankment next to the cauld.

Follow the path as it climbs above the River Tweed through the grounds of Melrose Parish Church before arriving at the roadside. Turn right and quickly right again through a small gate and onto a path that takes you to the banks of the Tweed.

Keep to the side of the water and head upstream for over 1km and when the path eventually narrows head up a slope through a couple of gates and back onto the road just above Lowood Bridge.

Common Spotted Orchid

Good advice

You pass Skirmish Hill where an information board outlines attempts to kidnap the young James V in 1526 as he returned to Edinburgh.

Cross to the small car park and follow the signs for Lowood Plant Nursery. Continue for 700m until you reach a narrow path on your left that returns you to Tweedbank station.

Horse paddock

T9: Tops and Lochs

Distance: 19km   **Time: 5 hours**

Difficulty: 🥾 🥾 🥾   **Total ascent: 556m**

Terrain: Tarred path, minor roads, woodland and farm tracks, field paths, moorland.

Panoramic views of the whole Borders are to be had from the tops of the iconic Eildon Hills. Beyond, the route crosses high moorland past three lochs whilst keeping the Eildons in view for most of the way.

1. On leaving the platform at Tweedbank station cross the road and follow the sign for Melrose Link path. On reaching a metal barrier, turn right and cross the road that passes through Tweedbank.

Eildon Mid Hill

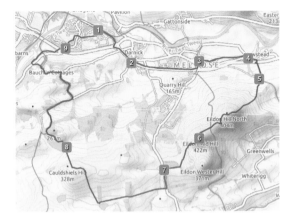

Turn left on the pavement to the second crossing point at the roundabout before heading over both carriageways. Stay on the pavement as it heads under a bridge to arrive at an underpass outside the entrance to the Borders General Hospital.

2. Head through taking an immediate right turn onto a path signposted for Melrose. Cross a minor road with care and follow the path on the line of the old Waverley route to the well-preserved but no longer used Melrose station which still retains its awnings, cast iron columns and detailed woodwork. From the platform take the steps through an archway to a small car park. Turn right then left into the town square before leaving on the narrow road on the far right that leads to Melrose Abbey.

3. On reaching the Abbey take the path signposted for Priorswalk as it runs alongside the impressive ruins into a public park. Keep left into a housing estate and follow signs for the Borders Abbey Way (BAW). Just beyond a row of garages join a narrow path

in front of houses and continue until you meet a stable block close to Newstead, the oldest inhabited village in Scotland. Turn left and head downhill.

Lillies on Bowden reservoir

4. After a few metres head uphill still on the BAW. Keep right at the top and pass under both an old rail bridge and the road, keeping to the right of the metal barrier. At the top of the slope stay left and left again as you pass through a large farm gate onto a track that runs uphill between horse paddocks. On meeting the road turn right.

5. Within 100m turn left uphill next to a grassy bank. Pass through a gate where you pick up waymarkers for the Eildon Hills and continue uphill on this well constructed path keeping right at the first waymarker.

This is a very steep section that delivers you to the flat top of the North Eildon. Use the track to the right of the cairn to head downhill towards the saddle.

Keep straight on and begin your ascent of the Mid Eildon ignoring the path on your left. The hill is 422m high and has a viewpoint indicator erected in 1927 which is dedicated to Sir Walter Scott who would marvel at the beauty of the Border countryside from this spot.

Rising 422m above the Tweed Valley, the Eildons were Sir Walter Scott's "delectable mountains", visible from his nearby Abbotsford House. The heather-clad tops featured in his poem *The Lay of the Last Minstrel* where the wizard Michael Scott splits the Eildons into three peaks with a malign spirit.

6. Pass the trig point and head down hill on a narrow track. On the lower reaches, off to your left, is the 'Little Hill' the remains of an extinct volcanic vent. Pass through a wooden gate and follow the path across a field to a gate in the bottom far-right corner. Keep to the

Summit of Mid Eildon

Bowden Reservoir

farm track as it passes Bowden Reservoir, a popular private fishing spot in the shadow of the Eildons. The game fish in the reservoir attract otters from the Tweed, who travel over 50km a night before attempting to scale the water's defences. The route allows for a short diversion around the reservoir or a visit to Eildon Wester Hill (see insert map overleaf).

7. On reaching the road turn left and continue for about 500m before turning right onto a farm track (take care, no pavement on this fast section of road).

The Eildons are sometimes thought to be extinct volcanoes but are in fact the eroded remains of basaltic intrusions from 350 million years ago. The only real sign of a volcano is the often overlooked fourth Eildon, the Little Hill. This is a volcanic vent that lies between the West and Mid Hill which has been inactive now for 350 million years.

Variations to this route include continuing to the smaller of the Eildon Hills (Wester Hill) or taking the path around Bowden Reservoir. The main route can be easily returned to from either deviation.

Pass through a couple of farm gates until you reach Lady Moss Loch, a former marsh and now a permanent loch, where mute and whooper swans and other waterfowl nest in the spring.

Continue into a large field and head diagonally uphill over a small earthwork to a gate in the top corner. There are often cattle

Swans on Lady Moss Loch

in this field so be aware and give them a wide berth. Negotiate three small gates into another field on your right. Head uphill through scrub land with a wall on your left.

Keeping you right – or left!

On meeting a fingerpost at the intersection of two fields, pass through the gate and turn right for a few metres before heading diagonally left across this rough moorland. Head for the small hilltop, Cauldshiels Hill, in front of you where there are the remains of an old hill fort.

When you reach a farm gate do not continue towards the fort, instead turn right and begin the steep descent to Cauldshiels Loch. Keep close to the stone dyke and the loch will appear below you. Drop to the water's edge, turn right and enter woodland through a swing gate.

8. Follow the path that edges the water and leave the woodland through a gate onto a farm track. Follow this as it loops down to a single-track road where you re-join the BAW. Turn right

Cauldshiels Loch

and continue to the first junction where you turn left, still on the BAW. Continue to a fingerpost just beyond a large cattle shed, that directs you off the BAW through a small woodland of yew trees planted by Sir Walter Scott.

On meeting the road cross and enter Abbotsford Estate, taking an immediate right turn next to the gate post and make your way past the front of the main house and on to the Visitor Centre, where coffee and cakes are served! Head towards the car park beyond the centre and follow the path across a field to a roundabout.

Front of Abbotsford House

9. Cross the main road with care, turn right and head into Tweedbank estate. After a couple of hundred metres, just before a bus stop, turn left on a narrow path to the edge of Gun Knowe Loch.

Follow signs for Tweedbank and continue on the path as it passes next to both a shop and Herges on the Loch restaurant. Turn left in front of the restaurant entrance to join the path where you keep right and head through an underpass. Do not follow the sign that directs you towards the station, instead keep ahead, staying left at a path intersection before dropping onto a timber-edged path into scrubland at the rear of the estate. Just beyond the next path intersection, head up a slope before turning left into a line of trees that delivers you to the road outside the station.

T10: Hidden Waters

Distance: 9.5km	Time: 2.30 hours
Difficulty: 🥾🥾	Total ascent: 203m

Terrain: Woodland and riverside paths, minor roads, farm track.

Faldonside Loch sits high above the River Tweed and Abbotsford House and is a Site of Special Scientific Interest (SSSI). Its sheltered location provides a haven for wintering wildfowl such as mallard, tufted duck and goosander, while in the spring coot and great crested grebe breed here.

1. Leaving Tweedbank station turn right at the roundabout and take the pedestrian crossing to the other side. Keep left and immediately right again into the industrial estate, no pavement here so keep to the grass verge.

Faldonside Loch

2. When the road swings left head right through the line of boulders on the grass to join a path that runs behind sports fields. Stay on this as it passes close to housing and through woodland before emerging after 1km next to a busy road. Cross and turn left passing a road entrance before meeting a roundabout, head to the other side and through a gate onto a path that leads to Abbotsford House. Keep right and head through the car park, past the Visitor Centre and continue out to the main entrance to Abbotsford House.

3. On meeting the road cross directly to a small metal gate and follow the path uphill through an area of yew trees planted by Sir Walter Scott, before emerging onto a minor road where you join the Borders Abbey Way (BAW). Turn right and keep

Faldonside Loch is one of 94 Sites of Special Scientific Interest (SSSI) in the Scottish Borders. The loch achieves its distinction from its animal and habitat diversity. Its highly alkaline water body is due to the remains of marl (limey clay) deposits which were formed and deposited in the loch waters after the last ice age.

on this road as it rises to a high point before heading downhill, keeping right at the next junction to arrive at a minor road intersection.

4. Turn right here staying on this road as it passes the entrance to Cauldshiels Loch. On meeting a cottage adjacent to the track, keep right and very quickly you drop to a rough farm track with Faldonside Loch below you. Keep a lookout for red squirrels in this area.

5. The track forks at the bottom of this section, turn right uphill before entering a field over a stile. Take an immediate left turn and head down the side of this field before joining a grass path.

Follow this path past the field entrance and continue beside the wall until you meet a small gate that takes you out through woodland to the road. Cross and follow a path into the trees before quickly turning left on a wider path that takes you to the end of the woodland. You are now back in the grounds of Abbotsford House.

6. On meeting this point, close to a burn, turn right and follow the path

Goosanders

downhill. As it begins to level out a waymarker directs you left towards the banks of the Tweed, with views of Scott's baronial mansion appearing on your right.

7. As the path begins to return to the house keep ahead and follow a waymaker for Melrose paths across a field. On reaching the corner of this field turn right uphill and quickly left to join the BAW.

Yew trees are known for their longevity and ability to regenerate. Their drooping branches re-root when they touch the ground. Often found in graveyards they symbolise death and resurrection in Celtic culture. All parts of the tree are poisonous.

8. Follow the path as it loops under the road bridge and continue on the tarred path on the other side. At a bend in the path follow a waymarker for the BAW as it directs you towards the River Tweed. Cross a footbridge and follow a track that sits just above the water.

9. When the path takes you up from the riverside keep left and with the Redbridge Viaduct appearing before you (built in the late 1840's to carry the Waverley line), take the wooden steps on your right to the side of the railway. Turn right and follow the path that runs alongside the track back to Tweedbank station.

T11: A Painter and A Prophet

Distance: 10km	**Time: 2.30 hours**
Difficulty: 🥾🥾	**Total ascent: 199m**
Terrain: Minor road, farm track, woodland and hill paths.	

The small falls at Rhymer's Glen, once hidden from view in a grove of ash and oak, were part of Sir Walter Scott's estate and a favourite place of his. In July 1831 JMW Turner, the famous artist, visited Scott and painted a watercolour of the glen, now in the collection of the National Gallery of Scotland in Edinburgh.

1. Leave the platform at Tweedbank station, cross the road and follow the sign for Melrose Link path. On reaching a metal barrier, turn right and cross the road that passes through Tweedbank.

Turn left until you reach the second crossing point at the roundabout and head over both carriageways. Stay on the pavement as it heads under a bridge to the underpass outside the entrance to the Borders General Hospital.

2. Follow the pavement as it drops next to the underpass and head beyond the hospital entrance. Keep right at a fork in the road taking care here as

Track to Rhymer's Glen

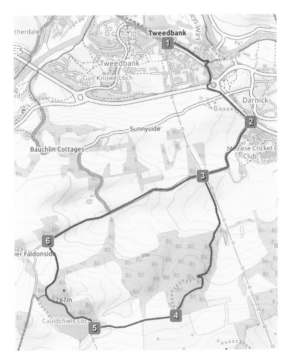

there is no pavement. As the road turns sharp right and levels out, you meet a fingerpost directing you left to Rhymer's Glen.

3.The roadway drops through a homestead before crossing a small burn. On reaching an intersection, pick up a Melrose Paths waymarker that takes you right towards the Glen. Follow a series of waymarkers uphill through recently cleared woodland.

Rhymer's Glen, so called after the 13th century purveyor of prophecies and poetry, Thomas the Rhymer. He achieved great fame after prophesying the death of Alexander III and was later immortalised in the ballad of 'Thomas the Rhymer'. In this he is carried off by the Queen of Elfland and returns having gained the gift of prophecy along with the ability to lie. The poem is also open to a riskier interpretation!

At one point the path turns sharp left crossing a footbridge before narrowing and returning to the side of Rhymer's Glen, a deep narrow gorge cut into the hillside with small cascading waterfalls. At the top, just beyond a wooden bench, the path reduces to a grass track that winds its way towards a wooden gate set in the wall ahead.

4. Enter and turn right along a path that runs between an electric fence and a stone dyke. Cross several duckboards before leaving this section through a wooden gate into a field. The path becomes less distinct here, stay by the wall and a more obvious track quickly appears.

Cauldshiels Loch is visible through the trees as the path descends and access to the side of the loch can be had at the bottom through a small gate.

Clear directions

5. Follow the path that edges the water and leave the surrounding woodland through a gate onto a farm track. Follow this as it loops down to a single-track road where you re-join the BAW

145

At one time it was believed that a mighty water bull lived deep within Cauldshiels Loch. It would leap from the surface emitting a tremendous roar that shook the surrounding hills. Keep your eyes and ears peeled!

6. Turn right and follow this minor road for 2.5km passing the turning you took earlier towards Rhymer's Glen. Enjoy splendid views of the Eildon Hills as you walk this section of narrow country road.

Continue downhill past the hospital entrance and retrace your steps back to Tweedbank station.

The Eildons in Springtime

"Still as I view each well known scene,
Think what is now and what hath been,
Seems as to me all bereft, Sole friends
they woods and streams were left."

Abbotsford House

Inter – Station Walks

A floral twist

IS1: Walking Through Time

Distance: 16.5km   **Time: 5 hours**

Difficulty: 🥾 🥾 🥾   **Total ascent: 366m**

**Terrain: Minor roads, hill paths and farm
          tracks, moorland, stiles.**

This walk will immerse you in the Border countryside providing a taste of its beauty, wildness and history. The route can be extended to Tweedbank station by following route IS2.

1. From Stow station head downhill before crossing the main road with care towards the impressive town hall. On reaching this turn up Earlston Road until you reach a small junction, keep ahead on Hay Park Loan to where the road ends. Enter the field

Gala Water Valley

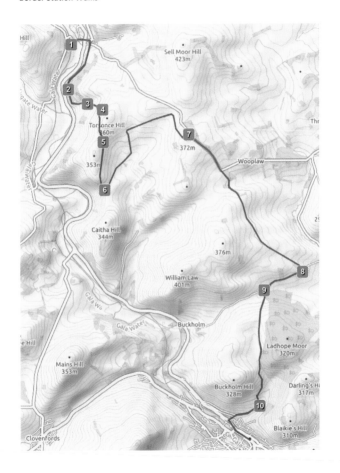

on your right through a farm gate onto a wide track and continue to the edge of woodland.

Head through a gate and stay on the path as it continues uphill through the trees to arrive at a farm gate. Enter and keep ahead next to a wire fence to a small gate.

Field gate

2. This drops you onto a tarred road. Keep left past some converted farm buildings before emerging at the front of a cottage. Go through a white picket gate and head uphill until you arrive at a pair of field gates.

3. Take the gate on your right and follow the stone dyke up this steep section of field to the farm gate on top. On passing through, take an immediate right and follow this well-defined farm track as it quickly gains height.

4. On reaching moorland a stone dyke with a field gate appears. Keep to the left of this and follow the wall as it drops to the corner of the field. Head to the small gate clearly visible in the wall ahead.

5. Pass through taking an immediate left onto a well-defined farm track. As you come to the corner of the field do not take the main track over the brow of the hill but instead pick up the less well defined but clearly visible track that lies closer to the dyke. Head past a large pile of stones and continue on a path that

151

winds its way along the edge of the moorland. The area is abundant with sky larks and their distinctive call fills the air.

6. Soon a cairn marking Bow Castle Broch will come into view. Continue alongside the wall until it turns then head up the steep slope to the broch. To continue descend on the shoulder of the hill and on meeting a path turn right and descend to a roadway that services the wind farm.

Turn left and continue through the wind farm for just under 3km to the public road.

Skylarks are a common sight on Border moorland and their sweet musical call can be heard from January to August. They nest in shallow depressions lined with grass with both parents feeding the young.

Bow Castle Broch in winter

Longpark Wind Farm - a dusting of snow

The exit appears just after a rise in the track where you take a left turn out of the windfarm to the road.

7. Turn right and continue on the road for 1km. As it swings sharp left stay ahead onto a road that is for local access only, but open to walkers. Stay on this as it takes you onto high ground past some housing and after 3km returns you to a minor road.

8. Turn right and stay on this for just under 1km before taking a left to join a forest access road as indicated by a fingerpost, for Buckholm Circular.

■ Brochs were up to 15m in diameter with a single doorway and were likely topped with a conical thatched roof. They had an internal and external wall containing a spiral staircase leading to different levels.

■ It is estimated that at least 700 existed at one time with the best preserved on the island of Mousa in the Shetland Isles.

> Scotland is on course to generate 100% of its electricity from renewable sources by 2020, most from wind power. Such are the weather conditions in Scotland that its turbines on average produce a higher power output than other European countries.

9. Take the steps into the second field on the right next to a parking area and head uphill to the opposite corner (path is indistinct here). Pass by a large cairn (Dobie's grave) and leave this narrow cleft over a stile and onto Ladhope Moor. The name Ladhope was given to the area by the monks of Melrose Abbey in the 16th century.

Keep directly ahead on the clear path that crosses this barren stretch of moorland. You pass over a stile and a burn before leaving the moor over a larger stile. Follow the wide path as it winds its way around the side of the hill before you arrive at a fingerpost for Buckholm Circular.

10. Turn left and head through a gate next to an old builders yard and follow this single-track road downhill, passing a cemetery before arriving at the side of the main road. Cross with care, turn left and continue downhill to a bridge before turning left to follow the pavement back to Galashiels station.

This route can be extended to Tweedbank station by following route IS2.

Pointing the Way

A snowy track

IS2: Bridging The Waters

Distance: 11.5km   **Time: 2.30 hours**

Difficulty: 🥾🥾   **Total ascent: 98m**

**Terrain: Tarred and woodland paths,
            footbridge, minor road.**

The walk takes you along the banks of Gala Water, immortalised by Robert Burns in his poem 'Braw Lads O' Gala Water'. Boleside is a stretch of the River Tweed famous for its salmon fishing.

1. Leave Galashiels station and cross the road to the Transport Interchange building. Turn left without entering and follow the pavement. Pass the first roundabout and continue as the road drops to a second roundabout, off to your left is an ASDA supermarket.

Old Tweed Bridge

Cross the road and follow the tarred path as it heads into trees with Gala Water below you on the right. Gala Water rises in the Moorfoot Hills and joins the River Tweed 2km downstream.

Keep on this path as it passes through a car park before reaching a narrow footbridge that takes you across the Gala Water. Turn left and stay on the path as it lifts over a small rise and drops you behind a flood defence wall. Opposite is an old mill now housing Heriot-Watt University School of Textiles and Design, an apt use considering the area's history of mills and cloth production. Otters have made a return to the Gala Water so keep your eyes peeled and you may be rewarded with a rare sight of these elusive creatures!

Dippers are commonly seen perched on rocks in the river bobbing up and down on the lookout for food. Gala Water accompanies you for the next km before the path ends at an old gasworks. On meeting the main road turn right and follow the pavement to a small roundabout.

Boleside

2. Cross directly to an area called Boleside and continue under a bridge and along a tree lined roadway. Wild garlic grows in profusion here during early spring. Below are fine views of the River Tweed and opposite the 18th century baroque Abbotsford House occupies a splendid position set back from the water's edge.

After 2km the road gives way to a path that winds its way down and up to the side of the main road to Selkirk. The path drops again, this time passing under the main road, close to the confluence of the Ettrick and Tweed rivers.

The Boleside fishing beat has been revered by anglers for generations and is one of the most productive in Scotland. Situated below the confluence of the Ettrick and Tweed rivers, the fish wait at Boleside until water conditions are right before journeying upriver to spawn. A 50lb salmon was caught here in 2013, the largest in Scotland since 1928.

A few metres beyond the bridge look for a well-trodden path up the banking on your right. Keep right at the top and head to the side of the main road, stepping over a crash barrier. Stay on this pavement until the bridge ends before crossing with care this fast section of road.

3. Step over the crash barrier and stay on the path that quickly enters open woodland close to the River Tweed. Keep on this as it passes behind a large house and narrows as it runs close to the river before entering the grounds of Abbotsford House, after crossing a small burn.

4. Keep left and follow the waymarked path towards the side of Abbotsford House and on to the Visitor Centre. Head towards the car park beyond the centre and follow the path across a field to a roundabout. Cross the main road with care before turning right.

When crossing the road bridge off to your right is the historic Old Tweed Bridge. A plaque commemorates the laying of the first stone by Sir Walter Scott in 1831. It cost £2500 to build and was restored in 2017. The arches of the bridge are decorated by alternating yellow and red stone. When the river is low the footings of an even earlier structure can be seen in the water below the current road bridge.

Meeting of the Tweed and Ettrick Rivers

5. After a couple of hundred metres, just before a large 'Welcome to Tweedbank' sign, cross the road to a small gate with a fingerpost that directs you onto the Solway Woodland Trail. Stay on this track as it winds its way through woodland close to the rear of housing then sports fields before finishing in a grassy area close to an industrial estate.

6. Pass the large rocks that edge the road and turn left. No pavement here so stay on the grass verge until you reach the main road with Tweedbank station directly ahead.

IS3: Walk The Line

Distance: 3.5km   **Time: 1 hour**

Difficulty: 🥾   **Total ascent: 31m**

Terrain: Tarred and gravel paths, footbridge.

A pleasant walk between stations that takes you over the River Tweed and alongside Gala Water where heron, dippers and wagtails can be seen. You encounter remnants of the area's industrial past while passing an old rail river crossing point.

1. Leave the station platform at Tweedbank, turn right and immediately join a path that runs alongside the railway fence. After crossing the Tweed on the Redbridge Viaduct the path rises away from the track side and joins the public road. Cross to the pavement on the far side and turn left downhill to cross Gala Water.

2. Turn right at the gasworks into Galafoot Lane and stay on this path as it runs alongside Gala Water.

The Redbridge Viaduct was built for the North British Railway in 1849 as part of the Waverley line and is now a listed building. It was closed as part of the Beeching railway cuts in 1969 but now carries the Borders Railway.

As you pass next to a flood defence wall, the remains of the bridge that carried the train to Selkirk can be seen on the opposite bank.

Just beyond is an old mill building now housing Heriot-Watt University School of Textiles and Design, an appropriate use given the area's history of mills and cloth production.

3. After 1km turn right at a station signpost onto

Heriot-Watt University School of Textiles

a footbridge that takes you back across Gala Water. Follow the path as it navigates the riverside, passing through a car park before heading into a tree-lined section with the river below you on the left.

4. As you emerge at a roundabout with a large ASDA store to your right, cross and follow the pavement before meeting another roundabout, adjacent to a large church. Keep ahead and within a few metres you arrive at Galashiels station.

> The Borders long tradition of weaving started as a cottage industry before developing into large scale production in 1777 when the Manufacturers Corporation of Galashiels was formed. The area now has a reputation for high quality Tweeds and woollens used by leading designers including Alexander McQueen and Vivienne Westwood.

Last view of the Eildons

INDEX